L. TODD KELLY

The Power Within

FIRE
plume press

Publication Services by The Kruk Creative

Learn more about publishing your book today at thekrukcreative.com

First edition

ISBN: 979-8-218-10511-2

Contents

This book is for anyone who's ever experienced pain on someone else's behalf—especially trial lawyers (who do it daily).

Praise

As a pastor, I am well acquainted with the concept of redemption. In fact, I often have a front-row seat in seeing how immeasurable grace can completely transform a person. That couldn't be more true of Todd Kelly. His story is truly a redemption story. Whether on the battlefield of life or in the battlefield of the courtroom, Todd has always given his all but this book shows how our all is often not enough. And it's in those places where we can come face to face with our humanity, and face to face with our Redeemer. I pray that this book challenges you and I pray it's a blessing to you, just as Todd has been in my life.

— *Joe Champion*
  Senior Pastor of Celebration Church in Austin, TX, Author of Confronting Compromise

The Power Within has exposed a truth in our culture about the demons that can control us if we let them. Todd's revelation about the impact that those demons had on his law practice, his marriage, and his family is too often hidden and allowed to grow, unchecked, in society, and especially in the world of the trial lawyer. As a fellow trial lawyer, I have seen first-hand the destructive powers that Todd faced, and watched too many succumb to them. This book is a must-read for trial lawyers, new and old, but is also an in-depth exploration for so many others to enjoy. I commend this book to your collection with enthusiasm.

The Power Within is a must-read! It's amazingly raw and authentic, and Todd is extremely transparent throughout. I could not put the book down once I started it. If you've ever felt pain, then this book is for you. Thirty years ago, I was feeling so much pain that I tried to end my own life after working undercover for the FBI for three long years, wearing a wire every day. This book will show you that most of us have some dark periods in our life but that there is HOPE at the end of the journey. I wish that I had this book available 30 years ago. It would have made a significant difference. I highly recommend Todd Kelly's book!

Todd Kelly is a gifted trial lawyer, a former Marine officer, a loving father and husband, and a dedicated follower of Christ. Todd's life demonstrates learning from your mistakes at a level I've never witnessed: he is now sharing his life story to impact and save the lives of others. Todd is living proof that the power of God can transform any situation and I salute him for having the courage to write this book. Suicide has reached epidemic levels in our country. *The Power Within* is timely, needed, and can change your life! I consider it a must-read for anyone.

Foreword

Ashes to ashes. Dust to dust. The hostage of Baghdad endured unspeakable horrors, but a phoenix arose to help vulnerable women who were subjected to the most egregious violations. Over a six-year period, the phoenix died under flames of combustion, decomposed, and was born again to shoulder the battle and pains for women suffering similar atrocities.

I was nicknamed the "Hostage of Baghdad," a title that no one would envy.

"In the deserts of Iraq, a war is going on against the enemies of America. In the heat and dust of the summer of 2005, a young American went to fight, not against Al-Qaeda, but for her own survival. She became the "Hostage of Baghdad," held against her will by villains of the desert, thousands of miles away from home in Texas."—Congressman Ted Poe, 2007

When I decided to speak out against the atrocities I experienced in Iraq, I crossed paths with Todd Kelly. Broken and afraid, I found an advocate who also became my trial lawyer. One that was fiercely compassionate and could internalize my wounds and trauma. He understood my desire to raise national awareness of the plight of American contractors victimized while working abroad for government contractors. All I wanted was for no other woman/wife/-daughter/friend to experience the nightmare I called my life.

He became the sword and shield. He put up a big fight—one which he felt was worth dying for. Arm in arm, we watched laws passed in my honor, which he directly helped me slay for. But ultimately, Goliath proved to be too big of an opponent. With stocks plummeting and bad press, the enemy was thirsty for blood and continued to victimize and try to turn us into pariahs in the media. With devastation greater than what we could mentally conceptualize, it was hard to envision a real future. He couldn't bear knowing the savage battle that I survived in Iraq, the miscarriage of justice in the courtroom, and subsequent rape in the media. Sometimes problems are greater than what we can handle ourselves. As my protector, it shattered him as it shattered me. However, even after losing the trial, his blood, sweat, and tears gave me closure by helping me make the world a better place for future generations of women. Little did he know, he was and will always be, my hero.

Jamie Leigh Jones

Prologue

Why in the world would anyone want to read my book? While I can't answer that question directly, I initially wrote The Power Within for two groups of people: Trial lawyers, and everyone else.

To the Trial Lawyers: because we suffer—often in excruciating silence.

- Weakness is unlikely to generate confidence with a public where trial attorneys compete for clients. Clients need someone who is strong and confident to fight for them when they've been hurt and now face a well-funded opponent who prepared for this fight before they ever caused the harm, and that is willing to fight a war of attrition to force people to accept less for their, often tragic, devastating losses.
- The Trial Lawyer remains quiet in his suffering, to project this image of strength and confidence. This often puts the problem into a pressure-cooker, causing the pressure to intensify until the attorney's desperation to alleviate it results in extreme reactions: bouts of drunkenness, drug abuse, and suicide, which are all too common in our profession. Is this cause one worth dying for?
- I write to you, my fellow Trial Lawyers, so that you know that you are not alone, and so that you understand that you don't have to let the pressure build that way. There is strength in admitting your weaknesses.

To The Public: because you simply hate Trial Lawyers, and I want to provide some insight into the people affected by your hatred.

- I believe that most of you hate us because corporations, particularly insurance corporations, have told you to hate us. These corporate entities have created a public narrative that Trial Lawyers are evil and greedy. Rather than focus on the fact that Trial Lawyers are the ones who actually hold those very entities accountable when their actions harm individuals, corporations and lobbying groups have spent a lot of money to convince the public (ultimately, our juries) that we are the problem and they have done it well. They have done it for a long time. Now, it seems that their self-serving rhetoric is simply accepted as a truth, regardless of whether it's supported by any factual background. It always shocks me when a family member of one of these entities asks me to help them. Really?! Against the wall you built?
- A few Trial Lawyers who advertise in front of their jet planes or other symbols of opulence have fueled the "Greedy Trial Lawyer" image. These few "bad apples" have really damaged the reputation by fostering a false narrative when one considers that the vast majority of attorneys do not live like this, but rather carry mortgages on modest homes and pay student loans and make payments on average cars. These few prove to be a disservice to the rest of the trial bar who has to stand in front of a jury and talk to them. Ego, here, has done damage to the profession. But these are not the majority of us. Most of us are truly good people just trying to make a living by helping others, whose lives have suffered because of the actions of another.
- There is a financial motive behind making you hate us, and call us names like "ambulance chasers." Follow the money. Who do you suppose benefits if you think less of us, or believe that every

lawsuit is "frivolous?"

It is in that fight that many of us lose ourselves, caught in a battle that many will, quite literally, die for. This is a battle that almost killed me, and shaped the trajectory of my own life. That is why I must ask: Is it worth dying for—or can you find the power within?

The Closet

L ate June, 2011, Richmond, Texas.

They're gone...the woman I have betrayed so many times during our twenty-year marriage has taken our daughter, Meghan, shopping. That is what they do when she comes home from college—spend money I can't keep up with.

The boys, too, are out for the day. My sons, Josh and Matthew love to visit with their friends. Probably killing aliens or sharpening their skills at the latest version of World of Warcraft.

Thank God they aren't home. If they could see the effect that these demons in my head have had on their father today...

The scent of single malt Scotch comes in wafts, together with the bad breath of a man who hasn't eaten in days.

I'm in my "dream home": the one I built to die in. I awake in the same reclining chair I have been in for the past three days. I've been lifelessly existing in this recliner in front of the noisy screen across the room mercilessly playing news recounts of the events that put me here.

I have not shaved or even bathed since I took off my suit three days ago. I stink of body odor and whatever food I have spilled on myself. I quit drinking when I finished the bottle of whiskey that sits at the foot of this recliner. Some of that adds to the pungent aroma of my chosen spot. Perhaps it isn't on the chair, but just on the gray terry cloth bathrobe that has adorned my beaten frame for the past three days. The very sight of me would have repulsed me a week ago. Today, I simply don't care.

I do find the strength to make it to the restroom. Or at least I believe I do because at least that aroma isn't sharing this chair with me. But as soon as I can, I return to the chair, I stare at the TV, and I wallow—just as I have for the past three days.

Then, there's the debt. The Stillwater Asset-Backed Fund has sued me for the $12 Million that they say I owe them. This is more than I could ever repay. I am financially ruined.

I know I should go to work. I can't face the people there. They were so hopeful for me. I was so sure I would win. I failed. This is what failure looks like.

My thoughts occasionally drift to the only thing outside of my children that has me questioning the inevitable end to this misery: Robbye. I wonder where she is. She stayed away from the trial that she had worked so hard on so as to avoid a scene with Marysue. That would have been an even greater disaster. I hope she's okay. I should call her. I can't. I should tell her that I still love her. I can't bring myself to talk to another person. After all, I let her down, too.

I sit in this seating area in the bedroom I share with Marysue, which now serves as my sanctuary unaware that the demons in my head would soon come to offer me an escape from this misery that I created.

I should call Robbye. I can't. Things will be better for her this way.

Any minute now and the demon's presence will be inescapable...

It will be better for everyone if I make this quick.

However badly I don't want anyone (especially Meghan, Joshua, or Matthew) to feel the pain of my departure, they'll be better off for it. They realize there's no escape from the burden of past mistakes. They'll move on knowing that I had done everything in my power to teach them that.

Most importantly, they'll learn never to make the same mistakes I have made that opened the door to those minions who won't stop gnawing at my soul.

I shake my head, battling the pain. I can't keep stalling, lest I draw their attention to my balking. But the movie keeps rewinding and looping in my mind all the same. News of my trial loss is all over the major network news sources: CNN, NBC, Fox News, ABC, The New York Times, The Wall Street Journal...and every other carnivorous syndicate known to the North American continent.

It's not just my name and my law firm's reputation that's been impugned. Jamie, the courageous woman I fought so hard for, and all of the women that she stood for by coming forward with her case—all of the women I was fighting so hard to protect in this public battle—no longer have a name and the sense of justice they deserve because of *me*, *my* pride, and *my* foolishness.

I feel their sorrow. Every ounce of it.

I feel their pain. Every minute of it.

I feel their suffering. Its entire weight bearing down on my shoulders.

I, alone, am responsible for the continuation of this pain...

To say that I had failed myself, these women and everyone around me would be a complete and total understatement. This was no superficial loss, I had failed in a deep, penetrating level known only to those who risk everything for what they believe in and come up short. I have failed as a lawyer, as a husband, as a father, as a friend, as a man, and as a child of God.

Speaking of God, I have ignored Him for so long that I am sure He is no longer around for me. I probably should get up and on with the task of ending this pain before I am denied any chance of sanctuary from this dark, inescapable, pit.

The time, I think, has come.

Alone in this house, I crawl across my bedroom floor and gather myself in a heap, cross-legged, on the floor of my walk-in master bedroom closet. My eyes fix on the object of my desire: a light green pistol bag with leather handles. The light tan carpet Marysue selected for this "dream home" proves to be comfortable enough. I sit, among the array of black, gray, and blue business suits, hanging above the western shirts and starched blue jeans hung meticulously in front of me. My side of the closet is a throw-back to a wall locker ready for inspection during The Basic School at Quantico.

My attention returns to the demonic noises in my head. *"Just open the damned thing, Todd! Do it now! Do it quickly and get it over with! End your pain!"*

The 9mm Beretta M9 pistol sits just within my reach, safely stored in its holster, inside my range bag. I know there are ten hollow point rounds of ammo in the magazine, which were created to do one thing: kill a man. The magazine is sitting loosely in the handle, not locked in place. I don't want to take the chance that a through and through will leave my family burdened with an invalid.

Despite my training as a Marine, I have never wanted to have firearms in the house where my children play—and where they sneak in at night after being out too late. The thought of standing over the lifeless body of a teenager who had snuck in late at night, unannounced, holding a pistol that was still smoking from the barrel, absolutely terrified me. Whether it's my own child or one of their friends, that is more guilt than I could ever face. The slight chance of a burglar is just not worth a child dying for. Perhaps this inevitable moment in the closet is merely another reason that I just had never consciously considered—until now.

One quick squeeze and the pain will end. The embarrassment will be over. The shame will be gone—*at least for me*. Those who watched my life unravel in such a public way will probably believe that I simply

4

found my most recent trial loss too much to take—and that my shame in losing so publicly was worth dying for.

It's a pretty pistol. I have maintained it meticulously.

"*Take it out!*" the demons scream in my head.

In obedience to the demons' demands, I take it out of the bag and draw it from the black canvas shoulder holster in which it rests. It smells of CLR and carbon, remnants of lessons learned as a Marine—I take care of my weapons. I take in that smell as if a familiar friend. This weapon has always fit so well in my hand.

I have become all too comfortable with her curves.

The Beretta M9 is the only pistol that I felt comfortable purchasing when my son, Josh, announced, at 21 years of age, that he was going to purchase a pistol, and asked his Marine Veteran father to help him choose which one he should buy. The first part of his statement was not a question, so I agreed to his actual request for help, and found my own pistol on the trip to the sporting goods store.

I bought this "nine" with the thought that shooting would be something I could do with Josh—to teach him since I had never allowed firearms in the house when he was young. The feared image of that dead child had been strong and vivid. The comfort that the protection that a firearm affords has simply never been worth a child dying for.

She makes it a point to remind me of our first date, at the range, with my sons. I have sure had some quality time with Josh and Matthew at the range. Meghan, too—though it's not really her thing. Josh loves it, and I think Matthew just loves to be part of the outings. I can see Josh holding his own 9mm weapon down range as I hover over him, teaching him about sight alignment and sight picture. I recall the pride of both boys as they pulled back their first targets with shots in the "kill zone" of those paper bad guys. Those photographs were treasures. Those memories, even more so. We liked to shoot my old British 303, too, but it was a difficult rifle to master.

I release the magazine to check the load. Yep, the hollow points are still in there – ten of them, so as not to tax the spring in the magazine too much. I slide the magazine home: locked and loaded. My weapon stands ready for a home invader, nervous misses and all. It only takes one of these to protect a home—or end a life.

I am well-trained on this one. "Squeeze. Don't Pull." I can hear my weapons instructor's voice echo in my head, recalling my time in the Corps. We were taught how to squeeze the trigger, and how to reload fast. I guess that second part now proves irrelevant.

This one, I can almost use in my sleep—thus the fear and the image that prevented her purchase for so long.

I half smile as I imagine all of the pain, embarrassment, and shame immediately disappearing in a puff of smoke. All of the guilt—gone! All of the suffering—relieved! I can already imagine the looks on their faces when they learn about what happened to me. Just a cliche.

I place my weapon of choice into my mouth. The Demonic voices engage, in soothing almost maternal tones.

Will anyone even care?

Won't this be better?

I'm insured for more than I'm worth, anyway!

Trial Lawyers do this all the time—I'll just be another sad statistic, right?

My family could use the money. God knows I haven't been able to provide it.

Why did I think I was so special? Why did I think that the world's largest military contractor couldn't find a way to beat me (even if I knew they would spare no expense, and try it without scruples)?

Why do I care so much?

Are you there, God? I try to interrupt...the demonic tones change:

He's not listening to you, Todd, you turned your back on Him years ago. Why do you call upon Him now?

Just pull the damned trigger. End it.

You are a terrible lawyer! You are all hype.

The whole world just watched you publicly eat it against Halliburton's lawyers. Who's laughing now!?

You knew they were better than you the whole time!

You know she was raped. You know what they did to her...and you just let them get away with it."

Now everyone sees you for what you are. Fraud. You just aren't that good!

Your marriage is a fraud, too. Your wife doesn't trust you—you've betrayed that too many times to count. All you're good for now is what you can bring home to her. And now, you can't bring home a damned thing.

You are, quite literally, worth more dead.

Your kids are embarrassed by you: even their friends know what you are. You spend way too much time at work or the dojo, anyway.

You're a cheater. Everyone knows you've been unfaithful to your wife!

Your parents are so ashamed of you! They used to be so proud.

You are a failure. Pull the trigger!

A deep shiver of fear moves within me as if a hand, frigid and cold, but invisible presses through my shoulder and forces my muscles to engage, clenching the pistol grip and trigger, nearly engaging the firing pin.

No, that is an eternal sentence in Hell! I plead as I try to remember my Savior.

What about Robbye?!" I almost beg.

There is no way you can ever be with her. Too many obstacles. You are just going to be miserable if you can't be with her anyway, right?!

How can you go on without her in your life now?

Did you learn anything at the ranch? Reverse roles.

How will Joshua and Matthew feel when they find me? Who's gonna clean up the mess that a hollow point will make of my brain? Will that image haunt their memories?

Hell, you don't even remember Lannie, and you have wondered about his death your whole life!

You bear his name—perhaps this is just hereditary.

What kind of an example is this for Meghan? I told her to never quit. Now, look what she'll see: Quitter!

What will this do to the kids who know me—who might still love me?! I am gaining resolve.

Perhaps they love you. They do not respect you! You will fail your own daughter just like you did those other girls! The demons retort!

Leadership—by example! Is this the example I want my children to emulate?

Leadership?! You just failed Marine! You failed every rape victim that you thought you could help! You have done more harm than good! Be a man—pull the trigger! They urge.

No—be a man, and face my mess. I cry.

"But what about Robbye?!"

"Another woman?" the demons mock. "*You know full well you'll only hurt her as you've hurt your wife and every other woman you've wooed. Do her a favor and pull the damned trigger, Todd! End this all now!*" they demand, more urgent.

The weight of many demons, as invisible as they may be, now completely crushing down on my shoulders. *'PULL THE TRIGGER, TODD! PULL IT NOW!"*

My mind races, frantically, as unbearable pressure and heat engulf my whole body.

My finger, trembling, closes itself tighter on the trigger...

The fight rages inside my head for about forty-five agonizing minutes. Then, I close my eyes...

Ego

My ego is too large, you say.
I now think that you're right.
My belief that it had been destroyed
Could not explain my plight.

If your assessment were untrue
Then your words would have no might.
And every time you put me down
I wouldn't feel the slight.

You've made me reassess my view
Of who I truly am.
And though it clearly evades you
My confidence is a sham.

Ego, yes, I have one still
Despite its beaten, ragged, shell.
And judge me, oh I know you will—
But you have not lived in my Hell.

So when you call me out next time
For all the world to see—

This low-life piece of filthy slime,
You hurt the friend in me.

I came to you a broken man
Whose ego suffered most.
Before I lost it by my hand
I was far too quick to boast.

I boasted of success and fame
And all the things I'd done.
For I knew how to play this game
But had forgot the One.

Perhaps that's why your words won't leave:
Why should I even care
If it's to His Love that I cleave?
Perhaps my ego's still in there?

So thanks, I guess, for calling out
This raging flaw in me.
And making sure it really hurt
So everyone can see.

The truth has reared its nasty head:
Ego's not gone, it seems.
Whether working late or froze in dread,
It made nightmares out of dreams.

The Home

This house was the culmination of the dreams forged between my wife, Marysue, and I back when I was still in the Marine Corps and the kids were still riding bikes with training wheels. Well, two of them were—Matthew was still in diapers back then. We had dreamed of a life in this home and had placed our hope in this physical space that, in the end, it simply did not hold.

Marysue had changed. I had, too. Certainly, my changed behavior and multiple indiscretions had led to the changes in how she treated me. Perhaps the opposite was also true. Perhaps it was a combination. Neither of us really addressed the cause and effect of where we had fallen in such a way as to have a firm handle on the answer to that question. What was certain is that I grew to be miserable in the marriage.

My kids, however, were another story. I adored them. Always had. Marysue did, too. She was a good mother to them. I was as good a father as I could be, given that I lived a "secret" life. But, I always loved them more than I loved my own life. Marysue had that to hold over me too. How many times did she have to remind me that *she* never cheated? I knew!

The twins, Joshua and Meghan, were truly miracle babies. They had been born at 27 weeks gestation, weighing in at less than two pounds each. Marysue and I spent several months in the NICU at Kapiolani

Medical Center in Honolulu, Hawaii praying for their lives. I recall holding these too small children and thinking that they were the most beautiful things I had ever seen. I understood, for the first time, a father's love for his children. A love that was worth any sacrifice. I would have freely given my life to save theirs. I made that offer in prayer often in those first, difficult, months.

Their early lives, after they got out of that scary place, had been spent in and out of medical appointments, and eating whatever we could get them to actually take. We just needed them to grow, and we were not above feeding them candy, pizza, cake, ice cream, or anything else that would add caloric intake. But as I sat in my misery at the home in Richmond, they were both in college. Both had graduated high school with high grades, and both were athletic. Meghan—a high school and competitive cheerleader. Josh—a black belt in Zen Do-Kai Karate.

Matthew had been born early, too—all of three weeks. His birth weight, a whopping six pounds, five ounces, earned him the moniker "chunk." That would wear off quickly, as he was thin and fit as a kid. Although he started Karate with his brother and me, he had a love for soccer that took him out of the dojo. Matthew was quiet and focused on video games. I could barely get him out of the house unless it was to ride in his golf cart (made to look like an all-terrain tactical vehicle) and shoot airsoft guns at his brother and a few friends.

These kids were the reason I kept coming home. They were the driving force behind me to this point. They were the reason I kept pushing on. There had never been any doubt that I loved them. I had been strict with them, and occasionally short-tempered, but my love was without question. They looked up to me—or they did before the affairs. But once they knew the truth about those...

Marysue had been kind to me during my miserable days after the Jones trial. She brought me my occasional cup of coffee, and whatever food she had prepared for the kids to keep me alive when I didn't want

12

to eat. She offered to sit with me, but I didn't want that. I didn't want anything except to replay the trial that I *"should have won"* over and over again. That, and I wanted out of the life I once thought I wanted. I wished that she wasn't being kind. I didn't want to be with her anymore. I had thought she understood that. Why did she hang on? I didn't want to be cruel to her, but I didn't want this marriage.

My kids, as kids do, were enjoying their summer off. Josh and Meghan were both home from college. Meghan spent most of her time with her high school best friend, Katelyn. Josh and Matthew were usually upstairs playing one video game or another which I had always been too busy to learn how to play with them. Thank God they had each other. I hated those games, but at least they gave the boys a connection. I wished they would spend some time outside—maybe throw a damned baseball! I knew that I should have gotten up to go be with them more often—that they wouldn't be home forever. I just couldn't. I could barely look at them, knowing that they didn't feel the same about me anymore.

Despite it all, I was—alone.

Broken

Broken homes and broken spirit,
I knew, but didn't want to hear it.
The way to mend the hearts unseen.
The pain they cause, acute and keen.

I painted a rosy picture of
A house shrouded in human love.
I failed to open up my heart
To the only One who could even start

To heal the brokenness inside.
But I was happy. No, I lied.
I was less than malcontent.
I forgot that love was Heaven sent.

I didn't have to be alone,
If only I would just atone.
Admit my sin, accept the gift
Instead, alone I sit, adrift

The Boy

I'm the eldest of two boys, raised in a loving home by my biological mother and the only father I've ever known. Some would refer to Jim Kelly as my "step-father" or my "adoptive father." That has never been his role. He was simply my Daddy—until I became too "adult" to call him that in public. Now, he's my Dad, unless we're alone.

My father is a man of unyielding integrity, who taught my brother and me that honesty is not the "best policy," but rather the *only* one. He was born to a poor family just outside of Houston, Texas, and was able to build himself up to become a small business owner in the computer technology field by first joining the Navy, and by applying himself aggressively to each job he took thereafter. He demonstrates work ethic, and dedication. More than anything else, my father has shown us what loyalty to family looks like. His love for my mother is still a shining example that all should strive for in marriage.

Similarly, though biologically Jim Kelly's son, Reagan has never been my "half-brother." He is simply my brother (or "my little sister" when I am teasing him—as we do). Reagan is four years younger than I am and grew up with me watching over him—not that he needed it. As we have aged, however, we have simply become friends and brothers. He has now had my back as many times as I have his.

My mother, Linda, is a strong figure, who taught Reagan and me at an early age about the strength of women while remaining tender in her love toward us. Though she gave birth to me at the age of 16, her wisdom was always far beyond her tender years, and she has been a constant pillar of strength in our family. Along with my Dad, she taught us the value of family, and let us draw strength from the stability of the love that we share. She managed the "Precious Jewels" departments of a number of high-end stores until she retired from Neiman Marcus after years of dedicated service. I often reflect on how thankful I am that she was my mother, and not my boss.

Lannie Ross Cross was my biological father. I was barely a year old when he died, so I have no memory of him. Jim Kelly is truly my Dad. Two competing stories surround Lannie Cross' death: He was either killed by local police officers connected to organized crime, after they beat him too badly for mouthing off, or he killed himself by hanging. These stories are equally convincing from family members I love and trust. I wonder about what truly took his life. That curiosity rears its head periodically.

My grandmother, Jewel Cross, and my grandfather, Jethro Cross, (Lannie's parents) were Christians who instilled in me a curiosity about Jesus at an early age during my annual two-week summer vacations with them in Camden, Arkansas. These were simple, God-loving people who loved me unconditionally—if not exceptionally—as I seemed to serve as a stand-in for their son, who died too young, even though they had eight other living children. This special love stayed be with me until their deaths in 1989. Though I have no memory of Lannie Cross at all, what I know of him is through the stories that they would tell me around a table filled with iced tea, dominoes, and a palpable love for God and family virtually every night that I spent with them.

A number of my relatives on the "Cross side" were (and are) pastors, including an uncle and a first cousin. I was always awed by that connection with our Father but did not feel that particular call in my life.

My father (Jim) worked for Bell Helicopter International during the reign of the Shah Reza Pahlavi while I was in elementary school. Mid-way through my fourth grade year, my family arrived in Isfahan, Iran, where I would spend four of my most formative years in this community with Persian neighbors. I do not return home to my native, Texas, until halfway through the eighth grade.

My childhood experience in a third-world country provided me with an appreciation of the United States at a very early age. The simple freedoms that we take for granted were not present, even in pre-Ayatollah Iran. Women walked behind their husbands to show their "place" in society. Their faces and heads were covered with chadors so as not to "tempt other men." Food was different, to say the least. Dairy was not as well pasteurized, and cream at the top of the milk bottle was something I had to learn to appreciate. My parents boiled our drinking water before we drank it to avoid diseases that our American bodies were not immune to. Peanut butter came from a blender of fresh peanuts—not a jar of Jif. Snickers candy—that was a rare treat, indeed.

The American School of Isfahan that I attended held an eclectic group of kids from all over the United States as well as other ex-patriots, and even a few Iranian children who were born to the wealthy, connected group of military leaders and royalty in this third-world nation. They all spoke English well enough to attend. These people, while they practiced a different religion from most that I know, were really very warm, and inviting. These people were my introduction to Islam.

It was during a summer in Iran, while my parents were vacationing in Greece, that some family friends took me and Reagan to a makeshift church that had been planted in our elementary school cafeteria. Family friends, Howard and June Brook, attended services regularly and took us to church with their family that Sunday. Though I was only a child in the fifth grade, I understood clearly when I heard God's call upon my heart for the first time. I answered my first altar call when the pastor asked if I wanted salvation. I felt His presence as I walked to the front of the church and received Jesus into my heart. I was overwhelmed by His presence in my body.

I was Baptized two weeks later in a church-wide service at one of the rivers flowing into the Caspian Sea, making my love of Christ and acceptance of Him as my Lord and Savior public for all in attendance that day.

I learned about the salvation available to all mankind that Jesus somehow found worth dying for.

With child-like faith, I understood that Jesus suffered an excruciating and humiliating death that He did not deserve, as payment for my sin—before I even committed it. I also knew that He was resurrected from death. I knew that He was still alive—I felt Him. I knew that He would return. I was saved.

Mom and Dad did not regularly attend church services, and my education regarding God and Biblical theology was sporadic, at best.

Despite our religious and cultural differences, we generally felt safe in Isfahan until about 1978 when the Shah was overthrown by Ayatollah Khomeini and retreated into exile. My dad knew we had to leave once we started seeing "Yankee Go Home" painted on the side of the houses of fellow Americans. Being from Texas, I recall thinking: *I'm no "Yankee!" I'm from Texas.* When my family returned to my hometown of Arlington, Texas, I was about halfway through the eighth grade.

Junior high school kids are harsh, and I had been out of the country (and their lives) for the better part of four years. I had no place in this group. I had to fight my way into acceptance—quite literally. As a "new" kid from a "weird" country with an unfortunately bad case of acne—at a time before medications were developed well enough to effectively deal with that embarrassment, girls were not exactly beating down my doors, either. This general lack of acceptance by the fairer sex would become a yardstick that I used to measure my self-worth for many years.

This weakness would become Satan's greatest weapon against my soul in my personal struggle to remain faithful to Jesus for much of my life after these formative struggles.

If girls give me attention, then I must be worthy.

As girls were not really happening in my life, I focused on my Boy Scout progress. I enjoyed the camping and the leadership skills that I was learning. Fortunately, my Scoutmasters were truly good men and not the type that would later give scouting such a bad name by giving in to their own demons and victimizing so many other boys.

I was accepted into an elite group of Scouts called the Order of the Arrow, and eventually attained the rank of Eagle Scout. I was proud of these accomplishments as I stood in front of family and friends to be awarded my Eagle Scout badge at my Eagle Court of Honor.

I played tight end for the James Bowie High School Volunteers, a District 5A football team that won a lot more than we lost. I actively concealed my involvement with the Boy Scouts of America, however. It was somehow embarrassing in this crowd of athletes whose respect I desperately coveted. The team was great. I was perhaps *slightly* above average, but did bring a lot of heart to the game—and normally left a lot of blood on the field—*albeit mostly my own*…Fortunately for my economic future, my grades were much better than my skills on the field and I would not have to rely upon my prowess under the Friday night lights to make ends meet.

One of my strong-suits was writing. Though I didn't know why, I actually enjoyed it. Like my Eagle Scout award, this part of my life was not "cool" so I hid this attribute from my peers, too. I thought I would like to be an attorney someday. Perry Mason and Matlock television shows and other representations that glorified the profession of law filled my mind with this image of a "noble profession" for someone who wants to help others.

I did manage to attract one girl in high school. Carolyn was my first love, and she did a lot to boost my confidence. What I didn't realize yet was that I was judging my own self-worth on how well she perceived me. We believed, at the ripe old age of 16, that we were, to each other, worth dying for. One Friday night, I came particularly close to fulfilling that call. Carolyn loved everything cowboy, so naturally I wanted to show her just how "cowboy" I could be. Sitting atop a two-thousand-pound bull seemed like a great idea from afar. I stretched my toes around the giant animal as far as they could reach. Leather glove on my left hand held tight to the rigging that my friends had cinched down for me to hold on to.

"Just eight seconds, Todd, then jump to the side and run. The clowns will take it from there."

I raised my right hand—signaling to the chute operator that I was ready. I wasn't.

As the bull jumped to his left, I followed him for that first move. This instilled in me a fleeting sense of confidence. *I've got this.*

When he turned back toward his right—okay, when he *whipped* back to the right, I quickly discovered that my buddy's skills at cinching down the rigging needed some work. The loose rigging slipped on the mammoth animal as I started to slide off his left side. My grip, more of fear than athletic ability, kept me connected to the bull—if only loosely.

Now, I'm not sure how many *real* cowboys out there can boast of having completed an eight-second ride on the underside of a bucking bull. I can. It turns out that getting off the ride while trying to dodge the hooves of a bucking bull is quite the challenge—particularly when you are dangling from underneath the angry animal when you do it.

If I timed it just right...

My timing was not right. The bull's hoof tore into my left abdomen as he dropped down for one more move. The excruciating pain was immediately overcome by fear as the angry animal turned to come back.

The clowns yelled at me, "RUN!"

They didn't have to yell twice. Adrenaline is a superpower and I was able to clear the gate into the stands where Carolyn sat, worried.

Carolyn was somehow impressed by the "manliness" of this event. I accepted her adulation. The wounds healed.

I would do that again for the pay-off, I thought.

Carolyn struggled with English Literature. I was in an honors class during the same class period.

I cannot let her fail.

I would do anything to help her.

Look at what she's done for me.

I dropped my honor's English to take English with Carolyn. That way I would be able to work on the same assignments with her and could tutor her that way. It worked. She did well.

We dated for the rest of high school.

I graduated high school in 1983 – 20th in a class of 640. I often wonder where I would have ended up if I hadn't dropped honors English. I moved to Austin, Texas to attend the University of Texas. I was still a good student—thankfully—because I did what too many freshman students at UT do. I drank— a lot. I was not walking in God's will, and had almost forgotten that I gave my life to Him. 6th Street was my favorite weekend location. My acne was cleared up and I'd found a long-desired form of entertainment, and perceived self-worth, in the opposite sex. Because I didn't look for my fulfillment from God, I received a substitute in the bedroom. But, as it does, that momentary thrill just left me seeking more—the satisfaction served as only a temporary salve on my broken ego. As any drug addict will tell you, the momentary high is too addictive to stop—even when you know the damage you are doing.

I continued to attend worship services on rare occasions, or when I visited my grandparents in Arkansas during the summertime breaks throughout my college years.

In 1985, I met Debbie, a sorority girl who was a couple of years my senior. She introduced herself by making a sexually explicit comment as she poured me a beer from a keg at a fraternity party I had no business attending. Well, no legitimate reason anyway, as I was not in the fraternity. Debbie and I started talking.

Debbie was a pretty, dark-haired girl who clearly knew how to work a room full of people. She was generally likable, and sorority trained to carry a conversation. She decided that my boots and western shirts were not the proper look for her significant other to wear. So I changed that without protest. Boat shoes and polo shirts took over my daily wear. *Anything* for the affection of a girl!

We had been dating ever since that first meeting at the keg, and started talking about "forever." I was not through with college, so I decided to drop out and join the local police force so that I could do what I believed I was supposed to as a married man. When I told my parents about my grand plan, they wanted no part of it.

So, my dad took me to a Navy recruiter to see about enlisting in the Navy, as he had done when he left home at the age of 17. This Navy recruiter, however, must have met his quota for the next decade! Despite an ASVAB score that would guarantee my acceptance, and my eagerness to enlist and move on with my life (and Debbie), the man directed me back to UT and to the ROTC program there.

Fine! I'll finish school. At least I now have a plan.

That summer I attended the Naval Science Institute (NSI) in Newport, Rhode Island, where I met my first Marine Corps Gunnery Sergeant. This experience, for those who have not had the pleasure, is not something I can describe in words. The best I can do is: Intense.

The hair was cut to a "high and tight." That was only the *first* change.

I survived NSI and returned to the University of Texas

During my senior year of college, I went through Lutheran Catechism classes and joined the Lutheran church. I did that (like so many other things in my life) for a girl (Debbie)—rather than for Jesus. I was quickly offended by the "closed communion," as that seemed the antithesis of what I thought Jesus preached. I attended for a time, but eventually left.

My remaining educational experience at UT was filled with a continuation of my walk in sin with as many women as I could coerce into my bedroom. My faithfulness to Debbie was less than complete. I graduated with a degree in journalism in 1987, and as soon as I completed Officer Candidate's School, I earned a commission as a Marine Corps Officer.

Now, I think, I am a man.

Addicted

As a boy I do not know the harm,
Awaiting just beyond the charm.
We chased the girls and thought it cool,
'Cause that's the talk of boys at school.

Never thinking of harm I'd cause,
Just like a wonder straight from Oz.
Emotions burning without control,
Or concern that I might pay a toll.

Ignoring risk, it just "feels right."
Perhaps another quest tonight?
Perhaps emotion, perhaps just skin,
That last encounter left me thin.

It's like a drug and I, it's slave,
I know it's wrong to thus behave,
But who's the victim? Where's the crime?
Besides I'm only marking time.

With each new partner, I am less
But I push on—despite the mess.

ADDICTED

Those closest to me should distrust,
For I have given in to lust.

I do not want to be this man,
But fill a void, I think this can.
So I chase sex as if my next meal,
Momentary highs are all I steal.

The Marine Officer

July 10, 1987, Quantico, Virginia.

I had just completed Officer Candidate's School (or OCS). Trained by another Marine Gunnery Sergeant ("Gunny") and a Staff Sergeant, my body was ripped, but my mind was even harder. I was a proud American that day! I knew that I served a country worth dying for.

My parents, Jim and Linda, and my younger brother, Reagan, flew in from Texas to be with me as I took my oath of office. I recall the pride as my mother pinned my "butter bars" on the collar of my "Charlies." The love and adoration in the eyes of my mother made all the pull-ups, push-ups, mountain climbers, and other forms of legal torture worth it. Her little boy had just become a Marine Lieutenant.

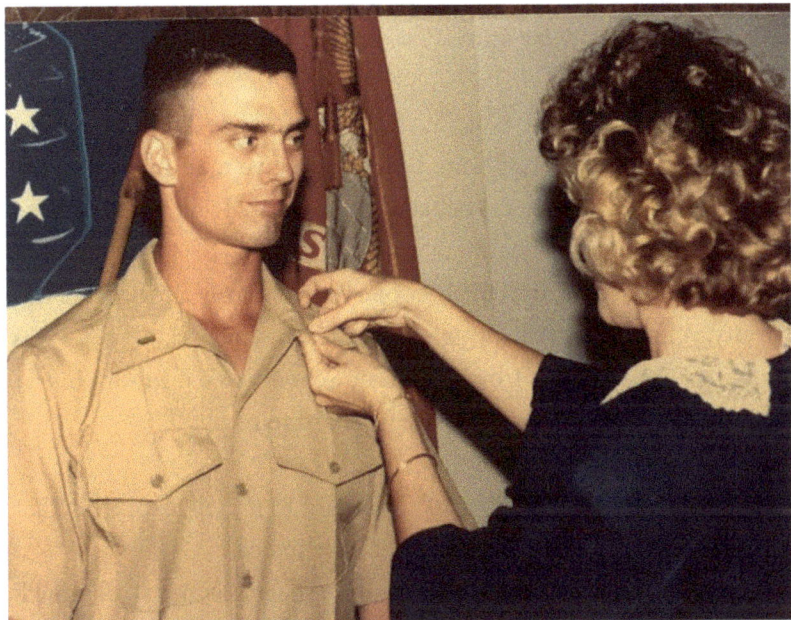

My mother pins on my Second Lieutenant's "butter" bars

Lieutenant of Marines. I sought that title for several years after my father convinced me not to join the police force. Now it had arrived. I would attend six months of The Basic School at Quantico, then out into the fleet to do—whatever the needs of the Marine Corps demanded.

My father had never been so proud. But I wouldn't fully realize the extent of that pride for a few years. Still, that day I felt the approval of this man whose approval has always meant so much to me.

As I stood in patriotic glory and the loving adoration of my family, I took an oath—a solemn promise to my country. An oath which I would take with each subsequent advancement in rank:

I do solemnly swear that I will support and defend the Constitution of the United States against all enemies, foreign and domestic; that I will bear true faith and allegiance to the same; that I take this obligation freely, without any mental reservation or purpose of evasion; and that I will well and faithfully discharge the duties of the office on which I am about to enter. So help me God.

At the Officers Basic Course in Quantico (The Basic School), I achieved enough success in my training, to give me some say in my career choice. I had friends I believed were worth dying for. Of course, they felt the same way about me, right?

I also met Marysue, the daughter of a retired Navy Captain. She was a pretty, young, vibrant, happy brunette. The first night I met her, I was out with several friends from The Basic School at a bar in Alexandria, Virginia. Her first words to me are not hard to recall:

"Are you a Marine?"

"This is going to be a good night!" I thought to myself, expecting that with a question like that she would be easy to bed.

Turns out Marysue was just making sure she knew the actual branch of service that my high and tight haircut was attributable to. She was smart, and she was attractive. But I had other plans for my life, so I really didn't have more than a night to offer her. She asked to see my military ID to prove that I was a Marine and not just posing. I showed it. We had a nice chat, then—despite my best efforts—that was the end of it...

A week later, Marysue called the duty officer for "Golf" Company—my company at TBS. She had memorized my social security number from my ID card, and used her father's military connections to track me down! With an unforgettable name like "Marysue," I knew that the duty officer wasn't kidding when he gave me the message that she called.

Several all-night phone conversations on a pay phone in the squad bay later (followed by exhaustive all-day training sessions), I started really falling for this girl. She seemed to have dreams and aspirations that were similar to my own; and as a bonus, she laughed at my terrible jokes. The sexual banter between us was intoxicating.

As the time for selection of Military Occupational Specialties (job assignments) was upon me, I had earned the right to select 9th among my classmates. I was told that I can essentially have any job I want in the Corps. I wanted to fly Cobra helicopters (my father had worked for Bell Helicopter, and many of my childhood heroes flew "choppers"), but my poor vision would surely have me washed out of flight school and the Corps would then just choose for me—according to its needs. Also, I had learned, much to my dismay, that the Cobra was not a Marine Corps asset, and I was not interested in flying for the Army.

While I could still have some influence over this life decision, I decided to select the MOS of 1302: Combat Engineer Officer. After all, I liked going to the field with the grunts, but what I really liked was blowing things up. I was like a kid with a new toy, only these toys were C4 explosives!

The idea of being a lawyer was not within my sights anymore at this point.

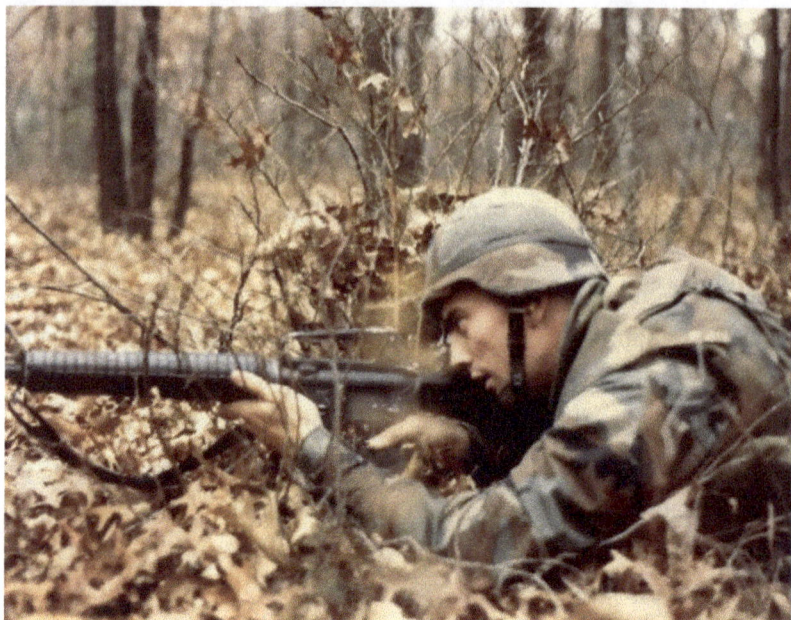

Training at Quantico

Marysue and I dated for the remainder of my time in Quantico. I frequently drove to Alexandria, Virginia, where her parents graciously allowed me to stay in their downstairs bedroom. Her father would sit just outside that room watching sports most nights, in a failed attempt to keep my hands off his daughter. We were in our early twenties and physically attracted to each other: no place was safe.

Our relationship grew into much more than the one night I had originally envisioned. Not only was I attracted to her physically, but we could talk about virtually anything. It became very comfortable. My friends at The Basic School didn't understand that this was getting serious and proved that by hitting on her when we would all go out together. My roommate, Frank, bought her a rose one night to gain her attention. So, naturally, in a barbaric display of testosterone and to ensure that Marysue never received the intended come-on, I ate that rose right off the stem. Made my point, but for reference: roses taste horrible!

My officer training continued at Combat Engineer Officer's School at Courthouse Bay, in Camp LeJeune, North Carolina. Serving with Marines I would die for is the most American thing I can imagine doing at this point in my life. Except on the weekends, that is. Those days were reserved for my conjugal visits with Marysue.

I got my orders before graduation from Combat Engineer School. I was assigned to go to Hawaii to be the engineer officer for BSSG-1. Then, it hit me: if I am serious about Marysue, I had better hurry up and marry her. So, in six short months after meeting her, Marysue and I tied the knot in a military wedding at Fort Belvoir Virginia. The wedding was small, but our families and close friends were there. (It was that or leave her, as I would get orders to Hawaii, and they don't put girlfriends on your military orders).

Everything seemed perfect.

I spent the next three years stationed at Marine Corps Air Station, Kaneohe (as it was known at the time) "K-Bay" for short.

I was assigned to Brigade Service Support Group 1 in 1988. The executive officer of BSSG-1 was LtCol Joseph Composto, a Judge Advocate serving in a fleet leadership role at the time. I am fortunate, as I will later learn, to have met him and to have had the opportunity to brief him on the engineer capabilities of our unit during a field training operation at the Pohakaloa Training Area on the Big Island of Hawaii. This man will eventually rise to the rank of General and will become the Judge Advocate General of the Marine Corps.

As I checked in to the Landing Support Company and was assigned to the Engineer detachment that I would command, I was overwhelmed by the responsibility. At 23 years of age, I was entrusted to lead 110 Marines and take responsibility for over $12 Million worth of military equipment. No pressure—but I did not let it show...

Gunnery Sergeant (Gunny) Robert Smith was my senior enlisted man and knew as soon as he laid eyes on me that he had to train another "Damned Butter Bar." Gunny Smith and I had conversations about the direction we wanted the detachment to be led. He knew full well that while I was the officer in charge, I could not do my job without him. I knew it, too.

As responsibility increased at work, things at home became stressful. Marysue and I had been involved in infertility treatment for some time. We both really wanted to be parents, but we had been unsuccessful. Every late period brought hope, which was only shattered days later when her cycle would start. We saw doctors, we tried "red light, green light" days (not the most romantic means of intimacy); we did virtually everything we read about. Still, no baby.

At work, I listened to the Gunny. I watched him. I learned from him. In doing so, my Marines become just that: *my* Marines. It happened subtly, over time. We were running in formation a year or so after I took the detachment, and I decided during the run that we would run up Kansas Tower (the historic hill where Navy radiomen in the radio tower first saw the Japanese suicide bombers as they made their way toward Pearl Harbor to bring the United States into WWII), which we affectionately called "KT."

But Gunny Smith contradicted me, "*No, Sir. We are going to run to the rifle range, today.*"

This was a point of no return: the Gunny had just told me, his Lieutenant, in front of our Marines, that he would not follow me. The fork in the road was both literal and symbolic. If we turned left (KT), they were following me. If we turned right (Rifle Range), they were not.

I directed my next order to the guide (a Marine who carries the banner that the entire formation will follow):

"*Marine, you follow me or you're losing a stripe today! That is an order, do you understand?!"*

When the Gunny turned right at the fork as he said he would, I turned left.

The guide stutter-stepped but followed me, and his lawful order—towards KT. The formation, in turn, followed the guide. We were running KT that day.

The Gunny turned around and caught back up to me at the head of the formation. He was grinning as big as I had ever seen him grin.

"It's about damned time, sir." My training, in his eyes, was complete.

At home, another task had become complete. We had just learned that Marysue was pregnant after our last round of in vitro. I was going to be a Daddy after all!

A couple of weeks later, I learned that there was more: I was going to be a Daddy—of twins. But our little world was not the whole picture...

On the other side of the globe, Saddam Hussein started a war in Iraq (the country bordering the one I had spent those four formative years in). This was the call that I trained for, I expected to lead my Marines into harm's way. This would need my full attention. I was ready, and up for the call. We knew the risk. We knew that my unborn children may never know their father. But we also knew that Hussein was using chemical weapons—even on his own people. This was the moment we had trained for, and we would continue to prepare. I have never been gassed with so much CS gas as I was during that life-saving preparation. CS gas is akin to tear gas. It is used to train our military combatants to use their nuclear, biological, and chemical defense gear properly. It is also used to provide some sense of confidence in the masks that we wear to protect ourselves. So, to ensure that we were ready to survive the deadly chemicals at Hussein's disposal, we prepared by exposing ourselves to this painful substance.

But the real tears filled my eyes when my twins, Joshua Ryan and Meghan Brough, were born early at the Kapiolani Medical Center in

Honolulu in June of 1990, at only 27 weeks gestation. Physicians urged abortion, because of the likelihood of significant medical issues and likely early death in children born that early, Marysue and I had to make a difficult choice that day about the lives of our unborn children. I hated this choice.

These little people, whom I had never actually met, were already worth more than my own life to me. I could not end theirs. After all, my mother likely received that same advice at the tender age of 16 years, and I am still here—perhaps there are days she doubts that decision...

Calling Artillery Fire

My ignorance of the significance of that early birth saved me from the full force of fear about what my children faced as a result of their prematurity. I was simply, by God's grace, completely ignorant of the risks related to their prognoses and medical challenges at the time of having "one-pounders." Ironic that I would later become a birth injury trial lawyer, well-versed in those challenges. I spent my evenings, every one of them, scrubbed down and looking at these little children that I loved more than I had ever known possible. My own children, who are worth everything to me. I prayed for them. I was willing to do anything for them to survive. If it were God's will, I offered in prayer to take their place. They were, more than anything I had ever known, worth trading my life for.

The focus on the survival of these wonders from God was stressful on Marysue and I. We didn't really see it at first, as we were both so tired from just getting to the hospital and praying for their very survival, but we were not focused on each other. I assumed she would just be there, and she knew I would be.

Although I didn't know the reason at first, I was ordered to the flight line at Pearl Harbor to assist in the deployment of all Marines out of Kaneohe into the theater of operations in Iraq for what would be Operation Desert Storm and Desert Shield. As a detachment commander for the company responsible for logistics, that role was not unusual. I eventually load *my* Marines on a plane destined for the combat zone with an honest promise to them that I was three days behind them. We all know that this is a mission worth dying for.

"*See you in country, Gunny,*" are the last words I spoke to the man who had devoted so much time to train me as a young lieutenant, not knowing if we would be reconnected "in country," or ever.

I made my way back to the makeshift flight line office in my shipping container and watch my Marines ascend into the blue Hawaiian sky. I could still see the plane in the air when my relief, a lieutenant, ironically also named Smith, walked in. *"The colonel wants to see you, Kelly."* My heart sank. I knew what it meant: I wouldn't be keeping that promise I just made to the Gunny.

"I can still see 'em," I urged Lieutenant Smith about *my* Marines—as if he could have somehow controlled the decision that the colonel had clearly already made.

I plead my case with the colonel about my Marines and how I needed to be with them, but he was unrelenting in his decision to leave me behind.

"You have two babies in the NICU, Lieutenant," he explained. *"They need you, and I don't need a distracted officer in the field."*

"I won't ask to come home, sir!"

"And I'm not asking you to stay, Lieutenant."

Again, God's grace—though I could not see it. Instead, I viewed it at that moment as anything but. I served *during* Desert Shield and Desert Storm—but not *in* it. I was, admittedly, bitter about that decision that I didn't have a say in.

After almost eight long and trying months, my Marines returned from the desert in Iraq to Hawaii and let me know that they always knew my heart—and that I wanted to be with them. I am dedicated to the Corps. I was a "lifer"—or so I still thought.

Semper Fi

The sweat-stained faces of determined men
Surround them like a lion's den.
The objective lies in plain view now.
The enemy does not know how.

Training days in Quantico
Were long and cold—with ice and snow.
We knew we wouldn't spend our life
Without some wear, some toil, some strife.

We understood that the price some paid
For freedom was one we'd freely trade.
Sacrifice, Esprit de Corps
Were what we wanted, and what's more...

We flew our colors high and proud.
We teased, we taunted, we yelled out loud.
The life we chose was not of ease.
But rather one to pay for peace.

Raised in this land where freedom rings,
We understood we'd feel the stings.

We knew when we cried "Semper Fi,"
That some of us were meant to die.

But not this Jarhead, not today.
I never thought that price I'd pay.
But our brothers, sisters, I knew they might.
And for their lives agree to fight.

So sleep in peace beloved land.
We are prepared to fight in sand.
Lay down your head and know you'll wake.
The other lives are what we'll take.

My brother warriors, train today,
So that we forge and make a way.
That freedom for our fellow man
Is bought because we care, we can.

All enemies from there or here,
Let me make this very clear:
For freedom we know some must die.
U.S. Marines. Semper Fi.

Second Lieutenant Lannie T. Kelly

The Law Student

I was re-assigned to Cherry Point, North Carolina, as the Engineer Officer for Marine Wing Support Squadron 271. While serving in this capacity, I applied to the Marine Corps Funded Law Education Program, (for a third time). I had no idea when I first accepted my commission that becoming an attorney through the Marine Corps was even an option. It now appeared that I had an opportunity to fulfill my childhood dream of being a lawyer—perhaps I could actually be the next "Perry Mason," or "Matlock."

It was hard to compete with combat veterans for the honor of selection to law school on this competitive program. I was, after all, not in the war zone during our most recent victory. This time, however, Colonel Keith Sefton, the Staff Judge Advocate at Cherry Point, North Carolina, wrote a tremendous letter of recommendation after I interviewed with him. I had a real shot!

Weeks of anxious anticipation passed waiting for the board's decision. There was a delay, for some unknown reason.

"Captain Kelly," Came the voice of a Marine Major that I had been waiting for, *"I have good news—and bad."*

My heart sank into the pit of my stomach, *"Yes sir?"*

"You were accepted." My spirit lifted.

"And the bad?" I asked. That part must have been a joke!

"We had to cancel the funded program this year because of funding

cutbacks, but you can still go—if you pay for it—on the Excess Leave Program."

"Ooh Rah!"

August, 1992, Carlisle, Pennsylvania.

I arrived at the Dickinson School of Law in Carlisle, Pennsylvania. Founded in 1834, Dickinson is the oldest law school in Pennsylvania, and one of the oldest in the nation. It was rich in tradition. I walk to school past the rich mahogany stairwell and take in the musty smell of the curtilage. The photos of barristers long since passed gave an air of distinction to the entryway and halls. This school gave dignity to the law in much the traditional way I expected.

I felt a twinge of self-doubt and insecurity as I looked up and down the old wooden staircase.

Am I in over my head?

Do I really have what it takes to learn the law?

Do I really belong here?

There was no turning back. I had been accepted by Dickinson—an honor in itself—but I was ordered here by the United States Marine Corps. This was my duty now.

Do your job.

Because I was still considered an active duty Marine, this *was* my new duty station. I took to this new job of learning the law like a Marine was supposed to: with determined vigor and a desire to be the very best at my new mission.

It was not lost on me when we sat in the large auditorium on the first day and are informed about the impressive credentials of this incoming class of law students: the valedictorians, salutatorians, Rhodes scholars, and others who sat among us. All top students from major universities. We were an impressive assembly of over-achievers. The dean instructed us to look to our right, then to our left, to take in the level of achievement (and arrogance) sitting in that room. Then, with cold, mathematical certainty that he clearly enjoyed, he informed us:

"*Half of you will be in the bottom half of your class.*" The reality of that harsh truth may have taken the wind out of my sails, but only temporarily.

Marysue, Josh, and Meghan accompanied me to Carlisle. It was close enough to both of our parents so that the kids' grandparents could enjoy some quality time with Josh and Meghan as I spent my time buried in my studies. Marysue was simply used to moving around as a military dependent her entire life, so she took this move in stride.

The concept of civil law was foreign to me as a Marine Officer. This became very clear in my first semester when Professor Michael Mogill, my Torts professor asked me if I understood the holding in the "Spring Gun Case."

For those who are not studied in the law, a "tort" is not a pastry. It is, quite simply, a civil wrong, normally based on negligence or reckless behavior. The holding of a case, for those unfamiliar with the concept, is the particular principle (of law) the case stands for. The "spring gun" case involved a man who had a collection of antique cologne bottles stored in an unoccupied shed on his land. Kids would break in when the building was vacant and steal the bottles and vandalize the shed. In an effort to stop these young thieves, the landowner set up and loaded a shotgun to go off when the unsuspecting thieves broke into the shed. It worked, costing one of the young thieves half his leg.

"*Yes, I know the holding.*"

"*Please tell us the holding, Mr. Kelly.*"

The Marine in me responded, "*Aim two feet higher!*"

Disappointed, but perhaps slightly amused, Professor Mogill explained that human life is always more important than property. Is it? Apparently, these thieves had committed a crime that I believed was worth dying for. This was the first step in a transformation that I never saw coming.

As it turns out, he was not wrong. At the time, however, I only knew that I wanted to prosecute criminals. Although well aware that other types of lawyers existed, I could see no other value for lawyers other than to remove criminals from our society. It would be years before I understood civil trial lawyers, and still a couple of years before I recognized that criminal defense lawyers are not the same as the crimes that they defend others of. I had a lot to learn.

Law school was stressful. As the dean has pointed out, half of us *would* be in the bottom half of the class, and some would actually fail out. These were people from the very top of their academic worlds.

Am I that failure?

Perhaps I was a fraud, after all? Perhaps I was just fooling myself to think I had what it took to be there with those people. My confidence was shaken to its core.

I started to change during that first year. I spent long hours with my study group. The late nights, occasional drinks, and long hours of study had the four of us leaning on each other quite a bit. I became close with all three, but when one of the women seemed interested in me for more than a legal analysis, my old insecurities revealed themselves again. She seemed attracted to me.

I knew it was wrong—I was married. Still, I couldn't help feeling the attraction of someone else's desire. Things at home had not been the same with the stress of the twins' premature birth, living through a war, then law school acceptance, and now the many hours devoted to the study of law. Marysue was busy with the kids, and I was busy with school. There was no romance there.

I had an affair with this girl that was quickly discovered by the others in the group. Despite the guilt that accompanies the affair, I did not turn from it because it fueled my ego in a way that I felt I somehow needed. As guilty as I felt about this affair, I didn't stop. It was an escape from the stress of law school and the fear of failure that has shrouded my once confident demeanor. It shrouded me in a false confidence about my attractiveness. It became an obsession and my primary focus. I convinced myself that I needed this. I even convinced myself that I somehow *deserved* this moment, these times of escape with her. I had turned my back on God, and I didn't even want Him to see me.

Marysue discovered the affair. Not that it was a difficult discovery, as law students tend to gossip worse than old ladies at a hair salon. We contemplated divorce. She even packed her bags and took Josh and Meghan back to her parents' home in Virginia. I held my twins as she packed her bags and wondered "what have I done?" I had never cried harder. But my tears didn't stop her. I deserved this.

I didn't believe our marriage could be fixed, so I didn't try to stop her.

Her words formed the only question she could muster: *"How could you?"*

I could not answer that question. I honestly didn't know, myself. I was also keenly aware that one phone call to my command about what I had done would end both my Marine Corps career and my chance at being a lawyer.

Instead, Marysue called my parents. When Dad showed up in Carlisle unannounced to take me to breakfast, I was shocked. Almost as shocked when he ordered coffee at the local diner we went to. Although he would make my mother's coffee every morning for years, he never, *ever* drank it. He said he liked the smell, but not the taste. Still, there was a black cup of coffee in front of him and he was drinking it. It was the first, and the last cup of coffee I have ever seen him drink.

The look on my father's face said it all. He was disappointed. That much was clear. But he was trying to help. He somehow understood that I had already beat myself up, so he didn't come for that. He just showed me love and acceptance. He showed me a father's love—when

I did not deserve it.

In the end, Marysue and I decided that our children needed a stable home and a lot of family involvement, so we decided to try to patch things up. It worked—for a time. It was difficult at first, she understandably didn't want to touch the man who betrayed her. We would have to work to rebuild this marriage. Trust was gone. That aspect of our relationship would never completely return.

At the end of my first year of law school, I returned to Cherry Point, North Carolina, to work under Colonel Sefton's direction. I was extremely honored and excited to work under the man who had opened the door to allow me to finally fulfill my dream of being a lawyer.

Colonel Sefton allowed me to work with the prosecutors and even permitted me to personally prosecute a few of those "scum bags" who had the audacity to violate the Uniform Code of Military Justice while wearing the uniform I value so highly. Odd that I could still be so judgmental, given the sins (adultery is a crime, actually, under the Uniform Code of Military Justice) that I was committing in law school.

I returned to Dickinson for my second year of law school. Again, I worked hard and was selected to compete on trial and appellate moot teams, and on the Jessup International Law Moot Court Team. I was even elected to serve on the student bar association as a class representative! I was gaining confidence in my knowledge of the law almost daily, making my way to being the best prosecutor I could be. However, my confidence in my own human morality was waning. After all, how could I profess to love my family and yet betray them? What kind of a man does that? I buried those feelings of self-loathing. They were not productive, and I was building an impressive law student resume.

In the summer before my third (and final) year of law school, I served my "summer fun" duty at Quantico, Virginia, which exposed me to some pretty mundane issues like people suing for money against the military exchange, vehicle crashes, and a number of other civil law issues that I simply didn't care about. I didn't understand the devastation that can come from a civil wrong—yet.

In my third year of law school, I was selected for an internship with the Cumberland County District Attorney's office. I was assigned to work with Jonathan Birbeck, a Senior Assistant District Attorney whom I had watched in a trial during one of our class trips to the courthouse—someone whose courtroom skill I admired greatly. Jon even lets me prosecute some of the misdemeanor cases completely on my own—letting me put some pretty evil prostitutes and marijuana users in jail.

The first prostitute that I came up against at a preliminary hearing had been picked up in a sting operation by an undercover cop. He posed as a "John" and arrested her when she named her price. Expecting Julia Roberts from *Pretty Woman* to walk into the courtroom that day, I prepared myself to hold back my own prurient interests in this woman. That was not necessary. I was surprised to see the appearance of the woman as she walked in. Years of methamphetamine and cocaine use, combined with living on the streets had taken their toll on this poor soul that had long since lost any pleasant physical attributes. Instead, I wondered "how could anyone find that attractive enough to pay for it?" Though barely coherent enough to speak, she was left to defend herself. After she was confined to await bail or trial, the DA's office congratulated me for winning my first hearing. I felt like a real lawyer!

Today, with the benefit of hindsight, I am ashamed to have taken part in the human tragedy that these children of God endured. I am even more ashamed that I thought I had the right to judge this unfortunate woman. That right was never mine.

Having "patched up" our marriage, I soon learned that Marysue was expecting our third child (and second son), Matthew Stewart, who would be born during my third year of law school. There was no need for fertility drugs or treatments this time around—it just happened. Our relationship, while still on the mend, was better as well. We made friends with other couples at the law school, and one couple even had kids the age of Josh and Meghan. This helped to keep our focus on the family and on our relationship. It also helped to re-kindle our romantic feelings for each other, which in turn led to Matthew's conception.

This is a good time for it, as the third year is much less stressful than the first two. The running joke used to describe the three years of law school is that they "*Scare* you to death, then *work* you to death, then *bore* you to death." Having a newborn made that third-year anything but boring. Unlike his siblings, Matthew didn't have to spend months in a NICU, and he was able to take a bottle the first day he came home. He was a healthy, happy baby, and he brought far more joy than stress. Watching cartoons with him in my lap while having a cup of coffee seemed to replace the need to be wanted by other women.

I graduated from Dickinson as a member of the Woolsack Honor Society. Top 10% of the class. Then on to take the bar exam in Virginia. The ultimate stressful exam—two full days of testing (some places have three). I traveled to Roanoke with my friend, Tracy Steele, to take the exam. Pass, and I'm a lawyer. Fail, and I am not. I wouldn't know for months.

Before I get my bar exam results, I was sent to Newport, Rhode Island to attend Naval Justice School. For three months I learned the ropes of being a new military judge advocate and, kindly, have a couple of months to get back in shape before we were to report back to the fleet. I was enjoying the courses, and the reshaping of my law-school physique, until…

I met a pretty, young Naval Officer in my class. She was shy but funny, and she was very smart. I was immediately attracted but kept my distance at first. After all, things were finally better at home! We ended up becoming friends during the 3-month school, and I fell for her—hard. Again I chose to ignore God as He told me to stay away. This one, I thought, I was truly in love with. I added yet one more to a growing line of sins that He paid for because of my selfish desires, and lack of foresight to realize the damage that I was really doing: both to my marriage and to my soul. I ignored all of that, and let myself fall for this woman—and I let her fall for me, knowing that we each had orders to different parts of the world and that this could not continue.

Then, still, without knowing if I had passed the bar exam, I was sent to my first duty station since law school to begin my work as a judge advocate.

Hawaii, again! I had actually been told "no" when I asked if I could go back. But I was not complaining!

Legal Fiction

The laws are written on these pages,
Handed down throughout the ages.
Brilliant minds stood in these halls,
Their photographs adorn the walls.

This musty curtilage and winding stairs,
Could tell the history it shares
With lawyers from the early days,
Who've changed our courts, our laws, our ways.

To stand among these hallowed walks
And listen to the well-honed talks,
I'm not so sure that I belong,
But I won't tell them they were wrong.

I've listened as professors teach,
I feel that someday I may reach
The confidence to stand and talk,
To truly walk this lawyer's walk.

Ego's here so easily fed,
But ego's better if it just lies dead.

LEGAL FICTION

Resumes built here, line by line,
What will I put down next on mine?

This school is building me up so much,
Yet, truly, it's keeping me out of touch
Reality isn't in our schooling,
It's hard to imagine the long re-tooling,

With time these legal facts and codes
May fade as ego then erodes.
But will the damage to my soul,
Leave more than just a gaping hole?

Graduating, honors, airborne caps,
We dream success and all its traps,
How foolish are those things of youth,
But time always reveals its truth.

The sins committed without regard,
Excuses that the law is hard.
Escape lasts for but a passing time,
It isn't worth the fleeting crime.

The Baby Lawyer

September, 1995, Marine Corps Base, Kaneohe, Hawaii (not sure why the name changed, but it was the same place I already knew so well).

I arrived at the Legal Service Center (this time as a Marine Captain), to receive my first assignment as an attorney.

I immediately asked to be assigned as a prosecutor—'cause that's what any self-respecting Marine Corps Officer wants to be, right? "...let God sort 'em out!"

The staff-judge advocate of the base leaned back in her chair, knowingly, and asked, "*I understand that you would like to be a prosecutor, is that correct, Captain Kelly?*"

"*Yes, ma'am.*"

"*You're needed in defense.*"

Only later did I learn that after a lawyer cuts his or her teeth in the courtroom by defending Marines charged with crimes, will the government move him or her to the prosecution team, thus ensuring that the prosecutors are consistently more experienced in the courtroom than their adversaries charged with "defending these scum bags." The United States Constitution at its finest—by Officers who swore an oath that the parchment on which it was written was worth dying for.

The team consisted of four Marine Judge Advocates. Major Tom

Hamilton was a calm, collected officer who would later go on to become a military judge. "Tommy Mo," as his contemporaries called him, was well-loved by most, but particularly by us—his defense team; Captain Kevin Mahne, a small, wiry guy who attended law school a year ahead of me on the Marine Corps' Funded Legal Education Program (he presented himself as a friend, but I'd later learn that he was less than reliable); Captain Arthur Wiggins (affectionately referred to as "AJ"), a large man with a laugh that was even larger, and one of my best friends; and me.

The "Dream Team," Kaneohe, Hawaii: Circa. 1997

The four of us made up for the disparity in experience with hard work and dedication to our clients. Despite our underdog position as the less experienced courtroom lawyers, our defense team won—a lot. In a satiric nod to the OJ Simpson defense lawyers, we started to call ourselves the "dream team." Arrogance at its finest—and we knew it.

The "dream team" was hated by prosecutors and by commanders all over the base. We were an island in this sea of Marines, and therefore spent a lot of our time both at work and during our off-duty hours, together. Friday afternoons were spent in Major Hamilton's office opening beers from the cooler that he brought in each Friday and discussing and reviewing our most difficult cases. As we learned, we bonded, and we won.

AJ and I were particularly close. Each time he stood duty on the base, he came by the house and had dinner with my family. My kids adored him and I treasured the friendship. He was my brother. I had not had a closeness like that with another Marine. This was the bond that was legendary in our Corps but had been lacking in my Marine Corps experience, until AJ. This was a brother worth dying for.

Captains Wiggins & Kelly in Blue-Whites in Kailua, Hawaii

I had the distinction of trying the first case in the Marine Corps regarding a new defense to the crime of "Carnal Knowledge," or, in the civilian world "statutory rape." The new defense, called "mistake of fact," was available, but the standard was high. The defendant had to prove that, at the time of the sexual conduct, he believed (reasonably) that the "victim" was at least 18 years of age.

My 19 year-old client was coming out of the enlisted club at closing time after a night of drinking when two girls approached him. The girls were dressed in mini-skirts and high heels and wearing heavy makeup. They appeared to have just come out of the club as well, and showed interest in continuing their night.

The girls had decided to lose their virginity to a Marine leaving the club that night, and my client fit the bill. The girls introduced

55

themselves to my client and his friend as eighteen and nineteen years old. The "eighteen-year-old" asked to accompany my client back to his barracks room to "party," where she willingly gave him her virginity.

She was thirteen years old.

It was my sworn duty to defend this young man, and his mistake of fact appears to be both reasonable and obvious, given his story. I understood this defense, and I understood from my limited experience that if I failed to act quickly, the truth would be lost. I called both girls. I told them who I was and informed them that I was recording the conversations. I asked each of them their version of the events. They set forth the *exact* story my client had told me. I now know he is innocent under the existing law.

The girls' fathers were both senior enlisted servicemen on the base. These dads were, understandably, irate at the sexual violations of their daughters, but were somehow even angrier about my call to them in the performance of my sworn duty as the defense attorney. These men expressed their mutual hatred for me as the jury handed down its verdict of "not guilty." The girl lost her innocence, but this verdict saved a young Marine who would have otherwise been convicted of a crime he had no way of knowing he had committed.

I was hated, even more.

Each member of the "dream team" was then assigned the largest case of our new careers. Four Marines were accused of killing a fifth—a capital offense. I was assigned to defend Alejandro Soto, the largest physical specimen of the accused. He had actually worked at the gym as his full-time duty! Alex, as he was called, was certainly not the mastermind behind this crime, and really didn't want much to do with it. But the government had its sights on him merely because he was so large, physically. Yep—that was the prosecution's apparent criteria for determining the mastermind behind this murder—who was the biggest guy? His participation, the prosecutors determined, was worth dying for.

I immediately asked for more experienced counsel to be detailed, as I had not yet been a licensed attorney a complete year.

Denied.

Unbelievable!

I wrote to the State Bar of Virginia (the only jurisdiction in which I was licensed at this time) to inquire as to whether the state that licensed me agreed that I was qualified to defend in a capitol murder case with less than one year of experience.

Of course I wasn't, and they admonish me so—in no uncertain terms.

I reported the Commonwealth of Virginia's well-reasoned opinion to the Staff Judge Advocate. *Now she'll have to assign another, more seasoned, attorney to this murder case, right?* After all, doesn't the accused have the right to competent legal counsel?

Two weeks later my answer arrived from the Virginia State Bar: "The United States Government has determined that you meet the qualifications to defend Lance Corporal Alejandro Soto. Accordingly, the State Bar of Virginia finds that you are so qualified"—or words very close to those—the letter no longer exists.

After some pleading, I was sent to Newport, Rhode Island, to attend the Capital Defense Course. The only thing I truly remember from that course was that I had one objective: keep Alex alive. Well, I remember a beautiful Navy officer that I was still in love with, too. She happened to be attending the same course. We had dinner and enjoyed each other's company, but refrained from intimacy, as we had seen the emotional damage that had done when we said goodbye the first time.

The key lesson from Death Penalty School was to do whatever it took to keep your client alive. There wasn't much practical advice other than that.

I got back to Hawaii and defended Alex the best I could at my level of experience (less than one year). To my relief, his life was spared. He was housed as a guest of the federal government for almost twenty years at Fort Leavenworth, Kansas—but, he's alive.

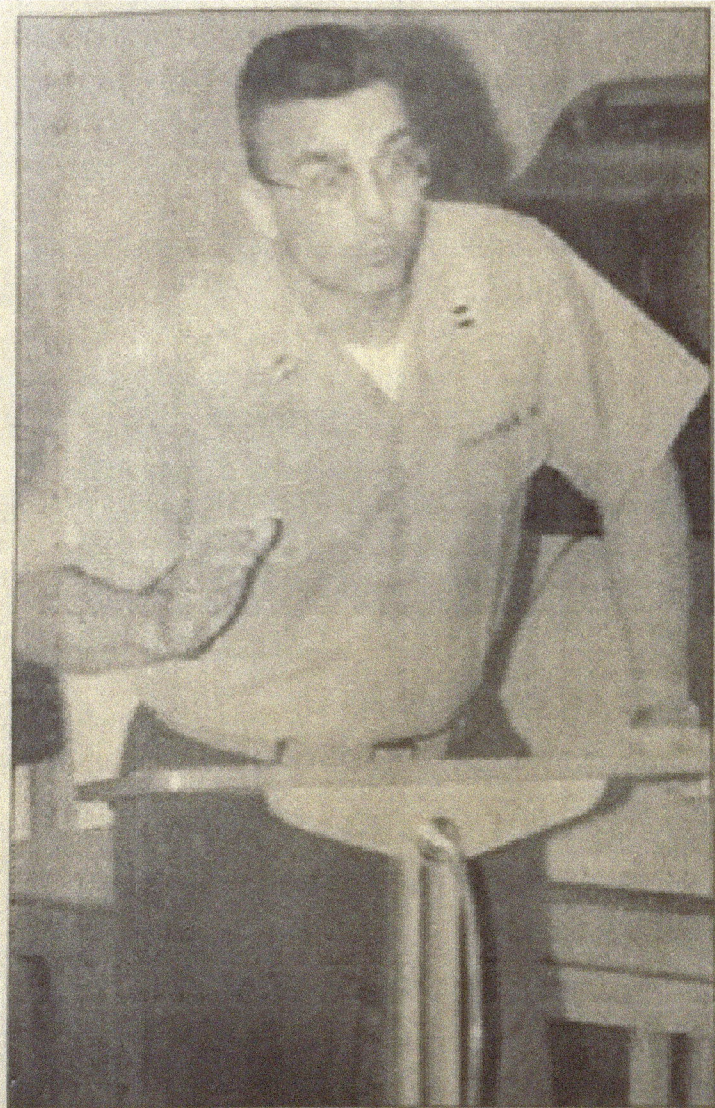

Cpl. Wanda Compton

Capt. Todd Kelly, defense counsel here, asks his witnesses questions to prove his case.

Although I thought that our team could never have been more hated than we already were, my wife was then called in to testify against a prosecutor who had been accused of sexually inappropriate conduct by the wife of the Provost Marshal (the head of the military police) on the base.

Marysue had been a dancer when she was younger, and Paul would frequently make strange, inappropriate comments about how "sexy" her *feet* were at social gatherings of the judge advocates on the base.

I could not understand how the legal community chose to put its arms around Captain Paul Aroujo, a prosecutor, rather than the victim (who happened to be the wife of Captain Todd Kelly, a defense lawyer). I understood why those untrained in the law hated me for the title I didn't request, but I couldn't comprehend it from those who took the same oaths that I took – and I certainly couldn't understand how they held my courtroom zeal against my wife, a victim of sexually inappropriate conduct. *Hypocrites*, I thought.

When Marysue refused to lie to protect Captain Aroujo, the fallout from her involvement lead to even more hatred among my peers in the legal service center.

Captain Aroujo was discharged for his misconduct. The repercussions of my wife's honesty will significantly impact my career.

I was hated, even more.

The Fewer The Prouder

The "Dream Team" that we thought we were,
The animosity we'd stir,
Defending Marines, most of the time
Less wrong than those who charged the crime.

Overcharging to them, a game
And so we fought with little shame.
Marines who'd made some small mistake,
Whose lives were now what stood at stake.

The arrogance of those who charged
The egos that it seemed enlarged,
Would they have found themselves so haughty,
If the world new about their naughty?

What of the perverse U.S. Attorney?
Who seemed on an unending journey
To bed as many wives of others,
Wives, or sisters, of even mothers?

He sits in his unshaken spot,
While destruction to others was his plot.

He'd laugh as though it was some game,
Yet his indecency not tame.

Right and wrong—such a simple thought,
But the world would change from what it taught.
Those who held the office—right.
The rest of us to fight that might.

To be correct is not enough,
To fight for right you must be tough.
For even those whose righteous cause,
Inspires hope, I caution, pause...

The fight will not always be won
By those who righteousness do don,
But sometimes when you refuse to quit,
Right may just pull out of it.

There is good and there is dark,
But if you care to be a spark,
Recall that sparks are bright, then gone,
But sometimes, fire lingers on.

Brothers in Arms

Marine corporal had been charged with stealing a government weapon, and his sergeant was charged with receiving that stolen property. AJ represented the Sergeant accused of receiving that stolen government property. I represented the Corporal accused of actually stealing the "government weapon:" ironically, a 9mm Beretta M9 pistol.

The Corporal had taken the pistol from the rifle range when another young Marine left it unattended at the 500-yard line. After he returned to the armory to check in his weapons, the Corporal stood in the back of the line waiting for the young Marine to speak up so that he could admonish him about protecting his firearm, which could someday save his life. When no one spoke up, the Corporal, realizing that the idiot who lost the pistol must have been at the other armory, panicked and kept the pistol.

The Corporal, afraid, took the government-issued pistol to his Sergeant's off-base house because he didn't know what else to do. That's where the Criminal Investigation Division finds the weapon and charged these two Marines with theft of a government weapon, though they were really only guilty of stupidity. Neither of these Marines ever formed the intent to commit a theft (known as *"mens rea"*). The absence of intent is a solid legal defense to a theft charge, and I was prepared to publicly embarrass the prosecutors, yet again. Perhaps that pride was my undoing.

AJ stood with his innocent client, as he entered a plea of guilty. Disappointed in that tact, I understood the risk and tried to keep my opinion to myself. I later asked my friend while we were working out together at the gym if I could speak with his, now convicted, client.

As he finished a set of inclined bench press, AJ responded, *"I don't care. It's over for him, anyway."*

A few weeks later, the former Sergeant (then a prisoner, reduced to the rank of private) was on base from the brig at Ford Island and I was available to speak with him. AJ was not, but I had his permission. The former Sergeant swore out an affidavit that substantially set forth the story my client had been telling me. There it was: reasonable doubt – in writing. I took the affidavit to the prosecutors in an attempt to convince them to drop the charges against my client. I was expecting a dismissal of all charges, given the clear evidence of reasonable doubt that this affidavit creates.

However, Captain Wiggins (he ceased to be "AJ" to me at this point) returned to the Legal Services Center and told others that he never gave me the authority to speak with his client. I could not believe it. How could one of my best friends betray me like this—with a bold-faced lie?

Like buzzards swarming the decaying carcass of a dying beast, the prosecutors saw an opportunity to feed. A formal investigation was launched into my "ethical violation." Within a week or so, the investigating officer arrived from Camp Pendleton, California, which brought a sinister joy to those in the legal center foaming at the mouth to end my career.

Though I had been ear-marked to take over as the Senior Defense Counsel ahead of the more senior Captain Mahne, the Regional Defense Counsel, LtCol John Canham, called me to let me know that there was simply too much happening around me to appoint me to that position, now. Captain Mahne would be taking that position.

Wiggins was, for reasons I could not quite understand, very friendly with the prosecutors who have had it out for me all along! How had *they* become so close, I wondered. Of course, I knew the answer but hated what it meant. He had chosen a side, and the truth did not matter.

Prior to the arrival of the investigating officer, I asked my "friend," Captain Wiggins, to come and talk to me privately, man-to-man, in my office.

I had been moved to the wing of prosecutors at the legal service center. The furniture was nicer, and my office was quieter. I missed the defense side, but the Staff Judge Advocate moved me to avoid any more issues. My office was now about 100 yards from Wiggins', rather than next door as it had always been.

The light-stained faux wood furniture was the nicest I had in my time in the Corps, and I was comfortable in this office, though not in my situation. The pace of my heart quickened as I heard the sound of Captain Wiggins' boots hitting the polished tile floors on his way to my office. I had never imagined that I would have to confront *him* like this. I envision him holding Matthew on his knee at the house, and all of us laughing at "Chunk"—the nickname given to Matthew as a comparison of his birth weight to that of his one-pound siblings.

"AJ, I thought we were friends! Why are you telling people that I had no authority? You and I both know that I did, and I am in some serious trouble because of your lies?" Getting the authority in writing from a Marine I would have literally taken a bullet for was not something that had ever crossed my mind. I simply trusted him—completely.

"Kelly, it's your ass or mine, and they're already gunning for you." His simple admission was all I would need.

He went on to explain that he knew his client had perjured himself in order to get through the "providency inquiry" (where you plead to each element of the offense, including the *mens rea*). He explained that he suborned the perjury because he didn't think he could win an actual acquittal, given that the pistol was found in the Sergeant's possession.

I now saw a man very differently than the one I thought I had known. A man who once held my son in his lap as we ate dinners prepared in my home: a man I had judged worth dying for.

After every prosecutor and member of my defense team had spoken with the investigating officer and each one had thrown me under the proverbial bus, the Colonel finally called me into the staff judge advocate's office to finalize the process of ending my career. I presumed that the SJA offered up her office so as to impress upon me the import of the meeting—as if I wasn't already convinced.

I was terrified that my career was about to be over (both as a Marine and as an attorney) and in disgrace, at that. I started to think that perhaps my cavalier attitude towards sin and my turn from God is why I found myself in this place. Perhaps it was. Perhaps I needed to wake up!

The investigating officer, after advising me of my right to remain silent under the UCMJ, informed me that things did not look good for me and that he was pretty sure that there was not going to be much I could say to change things.

He just read my rights! Are they charging me with a crime, too?!

"*I understand, sir,*" I almost whisper.

I could barely utter my next words, "*I don't even know if this is legal, but I know that it's the truth…*"

I placed before him on the desk a recording device that had been hidden on top of my wall locker when I invited Captain Wiggins in to discuss his rationale for perpetuating this lie in my office. I hit the play button.

"*You will be cleared of all wrongdoing, Captain.*"

"*Thank you, sir.*"

But politics being what they were, I knew that most people would not be swayed by the mere truth. Captain Wiggins was never prosecuted for his documented misconduct—a knowingly false accusation of a man that considered him a brother.

I doubt that AJ knows about that recording to this very day. I have to admit that until I was writing this book there remained a small part of me (a part that I am not proud of) that hoped he would read this to feel the pain he inflicted. However, God has freed me of that desire. As I write this now, because of His grace, I hope that if the man who was once my brother reads this—he will know (though it took me decades and several counseling sessions) that I forgive him.

I was then re-assigned to serve as the executive officer to the Headquarters Battalion—a billet in which to stash me so that I couldn't cause any more trouble at the legal services center. I withdrew from the corporal's case, so as to take the heat that was clearly following me off my young client.

The Military Judge, Colonel William P. Hollerich (dubbed by those who practiced in front of him "the screaming skull") heard my motion to recuse myself. Colonel Hollerich was intimidating to everyone who appears before him—especially those of us who were significantly junior in rank.

Colonel Hollerich sat on the bench in his courtroom; a singularly ominous picture of military justice from my view from the counsel table.

"Are you certain, Captain Kelly?" Judge Hollerich asked me, knowingly.

"No sir, I am not," I reply. *"But I have a duty to my client that I took an oath to follow. The allegations against me center around this Marine's case, and cannot help but hurt him."*

As the words left my mouth, I worried that the next detailed defense counsel would "play the game" at this young Marine corporal's expense. But, I convinced myself that I could no longer offer effective counsel.

"Your motion to recuse is granted, Captain." I won. It hurt.

Within a month, the corporal, a dedicated Marine who was not guilty of the crime he was charged with committing, entered a guilty plea to theft of a government weapon with my replacement defense counsel at his side. He received a Bad Conduct Discharge; reduction to Private; and six months confinement: the maximum sentence at a Special Court Martial. He lost all of his VA benefits.

At this point, I had become disenchanted with the United States Marine Corps. This, and the other miscarriages of justice, born of a system that was set up to ensure convictions rather than justice were not what I signed up for. I loved this Corps. I loved the men and women I served with. Was it all a lie?

Marysue had been a "military brat" her entire life, but we chose, through many tears, to leave my beloved Corps—and the only way of life she had really ever known. It was clearly not what I had believed it to be. This was the last in a long line of nails in that coffin. This Corps was simply no longer worth dying for.

I received an unanticipated call at about 4:30 a.m., Hawaii time. Marysue's voice brought me, slowly, into full consciousness.

"*Hello.*" She answered, then paused."*No, he's asleep … I will tell him you called.*"

"*Who was that?*" I asked, though barely conscious.

"*Someone named General Composto called you.*"

"*You just told the Staff Judge Advocate of the Marine Corps that I wasn't available?!*" I was now *WIDE* Awake!

I stammered, in disbelief at this daughter of a Navy Captain who was my wife. *She knows better!*—I chose not to speak that thought.

General Composto thankfully laughed it off when I was finally able to speak with him.

"*I understand you've had a tough time of it out there, Skipper?*"

"*Yes sir.*" I explained the entire mess (or rather, messes).

With an almost fatherly kindness, he asked, "*What can I do for you, Captain Kelly?*"

"Sir, I am only licensed in Virginia, and my time in this gun club is clearly over. I'd take any job in Virginia."

These are words that an experienced Captain of Marines knows better than to say. But I had no real choice.

My last nine months in the Corps were spent as the United States Marine Corps' Casualty Officer. My primary job was to assist the families of Marines who had been killed with their benefits and last rights. As a collateral part of that duty, I knelt to hand flags to widows at Arlington National Cemetery in my dress blues.

The first time that I don my dress blues for a trip to Arlington was memorable, not because of whom we are burying, but because of what the ceremony stood for. As the horse-drawn caisson stopped and the pallbearers removed the flag-covered casket, I felt a sense of pride for this Marine I never knew. I felt a sense of connection on a larger scale.

The slow cadence of that march, and of the slowed salutes added to the sobriety of that moment. After I dropped my salute to the casket, the first volley of rifle shots almost scared me out of my position of attention. I held on and braced for the next two volleys. Pride swelled with each one. Tears welled in my eyes as a lone bugler played "Taps" in the distance. I remembered why I first donned the uniform, and what my oath had once meant to me. It began, again, to mean something.

As I took the carefully folded flag and turned to the widow, she seemed proud. As I took a knee I noticed her tear. Then, I spoke the words I had been carefully rehearsing in my head:

"Ma'am, on behalf of a grateful nation, the United States Marine Corps, and the Commandant of the Marine Corps, please accept this token of our appreciation for the sacrifice your family has made for our freedoms."

Perhaps, after all, this nation was worth dying for.

The Cuts

Those we don't love cannot betray,
So the deepest cuts come in this way:
By those we've held in our hearts close
Those we've loved the very most.

When that one turns with "Judas' kiss"
And for the first time, you hear the hiss,
That one's bite does much more harm.
Is it because there's no alarm?

The cuts are deeper and the wounds heal slow,
In fact, sometimes, hatred will grow.
But as the hatred fills our thought
It's our own misery we've bought.

The trust we once gave out so free,
We now hold closer until we see
That those we would have trusted hence
We cannot trust—we build a fence.

This person did not cause my pain,
And though they try to reach, in vane,

THE CUTS

Why would I block them out from me,
Is there something in them that I see?

Or is it simply fear of love,
Because I've drifted from above.
If God feared mine, as I deserve,
Then He would never let me serve.

If I'm to love like He has told,
Then I must trust, I must be bold.
So forward as I must now travel,
I lay down my view—I drop my gavel.

Judgment wasn't mine to start,
I do not know what caused that heart,
To turn on me and cause my pain,
But I now choose to trust again.

The Awakening of a Civil Trial Lawyer

I n my evening hours as I finished my time in the Corps, I sent a resume, law school transcript, and writing sample to every law firm in Virginia, it seemed. I had each packet spiral bound, so as to stand out from the mass of applications that I knew must be flooding these firms.

May 20, 1998. Ten years, ten months, and ten days. Discharged. Honorably. A Major in the United States Marine Corps Reserve. Still licensed to practice law.

A "Baby Lawyer" no more, I then had to find my way as a civilian trial lawyer.

All those evening applications eventually resulted in a job offer. It was a pay cut from what a Marine Captain of my time-in-grade was making, and far less than I would have made as a Major, but I was desperate to get on with this new career, and it was certainly more than an unemployed lawyer would make.

The "silk stocking" law firm of Hunton & Williams interviewed me three times for one of their litigation teams. I wore my best suits and pretended to like sushi (it was a taste I would only later acquire, and learn to appreciate all too well). When they decided to hire someone else, I was told it was because my law school does not have the "pedigree" that they desired. I laugh at those "pedigrees" today, but it hurt at the time.

I found work as a plaintiff's personal injury trial lawyer in Newport News, Virginia. I didn't know that I had a penchant for this work...yet. In my interview, I told Robert "Bobby" Hatten that I was never more alive than when I was speaking to a jury. He seemed to like that as an interview line, but I had no idea that his plans for me were far from that vision.

The firm (at that time called Patten, Wornom & Watkins) made its name in the '80s, representing shipyard workers exposed to asbestos. These were hard-working men and women who had believed the lie told by Johns-Manville and other corporate entities, that asbestos was safe.

Many of these hard-working men were dying from exposure to asbestos, and even more, were sick with cancers or other permanent illnesses caused by this airborne menace. Even their wives and closest family members were dying of the same diseases, having inhaled the deadly silica when they dutifully cleaned their husband's clothing—shaking the invisible fibers of death into the air.

These jobs were never worth dying for, except to the corporate executives who didn't pay that price. These hardworking Americans' lives were simply a cost of business to the executives who cared more about bottom lines.

This reality was horrific enough. But the fact that Johns-Manville and the other manufacturers had actual knowledge, based on their own studies, that they were exposing people to deadly products, is what instilled the passion to advocate for the injured people in me. How could they?!

How naive I was to believe that morality even mattered to them. Money is all they cared about.

I soon came to learn that this is just what big businesses do: make money regardless of who gets hurt.

I distinctly remember one client with mesothelioma (a deadly cancer caused by only one thing: asbestos exposure). This woman was too young to have worked in the shipyard before she went to college and then medical school.

Her father, a pipefitter at Newport News Shipyard, had taken home scraps of the fireproof material to protect his young baby in her crib in case of a house fire. He was "protecting" her from the danger he was aware of, blind to the harm that he was causing with the material he was handling.

As babies do, she would scratch at the material, making the friable asbestos become airborne, so that she would inhale the nearly invisible particles. The disease, as it does, laid dormant in her lungs for almost thirty years—just long enough for the "infant" to graduate from medical school and begin her residency—before it reared its devastating impact.

Mesothelioma has a 100% success rate of killing its victims. But her daddy, arguably, got the worst of it—in a cruel twist of fate, he would live to watch his acts (intended to save his baby girl) kill his daughter painfully over the next two years. He would survive his own exposure.

Stories like these haunt trial lawyers. There may be those who can easily brush things like that off, but for most of us, the pain we feel, known as second-hand stress, creeps in like an invisible airborne particle with the power to devastate a life—one tragedy at a time over the course of years, until we eventually succumb to the damage.

These are the trial lawyers I know: men and women scarred by the pain inflicted upon them by uncaring corporations and insurance executives who consistently place money ahead of human life and dignity. Some have simply called it "despair," while others call it "second-hand PTSD." Many have found their lives not worth living and sought relief from the stress and pain of these stories believing that the relief from that pain was worth dying for—and often intentionally—at their own hand.

After four years as an associate with the firm in Virginia (which later changed its name to Patten, Wornom, Hatten & Diamonstein), I determined (wrongly, as it turns out) that asbestos litigation was nearing its end. I also appeared to have hit a sort of professional ceiling in my career at the firm. Not that it was a high ceiling, but the low pay of an associate was adding burdens on my marriage that were difficult to withstand. When I would ask for a raise, it was not greeted with welcome approval, but with analogies to people with lots of marbles. The stress didn't remain at the office but came home where the lack of income caused harsh discussions about who was contributing more to the marriage. I felt I had become merely a "wage-earner" in my own home—and I was apparently not very good at that!

My decision to leave was hastened when Bobby Hatten asked me, in my annual review, about how I felt about my work at the firm.

We've had this discussion privately, Bobby. Why are you asking this in front of your partners? I pondered to myself.

I answered his inquiry honestly:

"I would prefer to be in the action in the courtroom, and while I respect the work of the men in this room who have done that work and laid the groundwork for so many to be compensated, my true calling is in the well of a courtroom."

In response to my honest recitation of where my heart lies, Alan Diamonstein, in his deep, slow, South Virginian drawl (born of his years in the Virginia Legislature) was both flattering and ominous, as I knew it marked the end of my time at the firm:

"Well, Todd, I would expect nothing less from any self-respecting trial lawyer."

As those indelible words sunk in over the next few days, I made the decision to move to Pennsylvania (where I graduated from law school, and where the prestige of The Dickinson School of Law was actually appreciated enough to help with job searching). I had gotten licensed there over the prior year.

This time, however, I fully understood that I could not work for forces that stood against individual people. I had to work for a plaintiff's firm. I had to help the injured—not the large corporations that injured people without regard for them, then makes them fight for some small scrap of justice.

Baby Lawyer

"Baby Lawyer," what a term,
We want to shed it like some germ
That we have caught and cannot rid,
"I'm a lawyer—not a kid!"

But the term has meaning, there's no doubt,
When we first start, we have no clout.
As we are learning to find our voice,
Our clients have another choice.

They could choose a more seasoned speaker,
Rather than one whose voice is weaker.
Judge's listen when hair turns gray,
It seems all wrong, but it is the way.

I've learned that money drives corporate greed,
And in its wake leaves those in need
It leaves them broken, dying, dead,
And some will turn to me, instead.

Ego now turns into fear
As it is my voice these people hear.

THE POWER WITHIN

I am not sure if I can,
I want to help. Am I the man?

Learning of the money lust,
And that there is so little trust,
A younger lawyer's mind is set:
It's so much more than just a bet.

This "business" matters and lives are changed,
But there are so many deranged
That convincing twelve that we are right,
Remains a monumental fight.

So now for clients that I love,
And fear that there's no shortage of.
We take the fight to larger firms,
And try to bring them to our terms.

It's not for greed, as many say,
But just so ours can see a day
When justice comes into their lives,
To be with husbands, kids, and wives.

The playing field is tilted down,
As we look up, and all around,
Opponents, judges, are all chatters
But we will fight for all that matters

Crawls With God

I know that it is only God who completes me and that the only perfection I have ever experienced is in watching His perfect love forgive me and welcome me home. For some reason I keep finding a way to walk away from him, only to eventually hit my knees and crawl back.

While working at Patten, Wornom, & Watkins, I started to attend Sunday morning services with Marysue and our three children at Hilton Christian Church, in Newport News. It was an older church with an aging congregation, but they were very welcoming of our young family.

I was returning to a closer relationship with God and wanted Him in my life and in the lives of my children. The congregation was generally made up of shipyard workers and their families in the Hilton area of Newport News. Many of these people had been devastated by asbestos-related diseases that I saw in my professional life. Our family's welcome was evident, and eventually, I was even asked to serve as a Deacon. I was honored to do this in this small Christ-centered church. My soul was enriched both at work and in my faith. I had been forgiven for the stray steps I had taken out of my marriage. I was, for a time, complete.

But this was not my first attempt at a walk with God. While on active duty in the Marine Corps, I sporadically attended church services in the base chapel but didn't really consider myself a regular attendee. I prayed, occasionally, but spent no time in His Word.

When I joined Hilton Christian Church I again felt a strong connection to my Savior.

While I originally viewed these times as "walking" with God, in fairness, I wasn't mature enough to walk. In truth, I was merely crawling.

Jesus Loves Me

Jesus loves me, this I know,
But I sure wish His face he'd show.
I haven't seen Him in so long,
I am weak—does He hear my song?

I'm a sinner, and I know that's true,
But You said that You'd love me, too.
If You love me where are You?
Nothing I do reveals You.

If I read your word and pray,
You will listen, so You say.
If I call to you in pain,
You will hear me once again.

So, do You love me?
Say, do You love me?
Jesus, You love me?
The Bible tells me so.

I'm so busy, I can't stay,
I'm too busy to stop and pray,

THE POWER WITHIN

I'm too busy now, for You,
But there are still things that You should do...

Isn't that how this thing goes,
You grant wishes that I chose?
That must be there in your book,
If I simply took the time to look.

The Keystone Lawyer

After leaving Patten, Wornom, Hatten & Diamonstein, I worked in Pennsylvania for just over a year for the law firm of Cohen & Feeley. I was a personal injury associate and was fortunate to work with a contemporary associate named Steven Margolis. Steve and I became good friends. He was Jewish, and we had discussions about our respective views on faith as well as the practice of law that were both intellectually challenging and stimulating. Steve's friendship helps me to grow, both as an advocate and in my perspective of faith.

I was unable to sell the home in Virginia for almost a year, so I was forced to live away from Marysue and the kids.

During the week, I lived in a musty basement room that had been converted for the purpose by a retired Catholic Priest, who lived upstairs in the main house. This was all we could afford for me, given our situation. There was a bathroom in the basement, but it was just down the hall from my room. Living in this one-room space was depressing, in and of itself. I slept on an air mattress on the floor, which I re-inflated every day because it wouldn't hold air. There was no television. I frequently left this space unless I was sleeping. I did not like being there and resented not being in the nice home my wife and kids lived in.

I traveled to Virginia on the weekends to see them, but the six-hour drive got really old. This weekend obligation put an additional strain on a relationship that was really not in a position to take more.

Although I was working on some significant cases, my supervising attorney informed me that he determined that I was not ready to handle the actual trial on my larger cases (despite the fact that I had worked them up to get them ready for trial, and right up to the point that he took over the cases and settled them). The clients were well cared for. The partner who supervised me was well compensated, and I continued to live in a basement apartment away from my family, driving 12 hours per week just to see my kids.

Ultimately, I remembered another lesson that I learned in law school: my Texas-born body does not endure the cold well, and I did not like shoveling snow. Not at all. I decided to return to my native Texas in 2002.

I would only work for a plaintiff's personal injury law firm, helping injured people, so I sent resumes to personal injury firms in my home state, but few responses were forthcoming. Although I was becoming a seasoned associate, I was also a brand new Texas lawyer.

My wife's sister and brother-in-law lived in Katy, a suburb of Houston, and she was pushing for me to look in that area. Then I received a call from Jacquelyn C. Gregan, a medical malpractice attorney at a boutique firm in Houston, called Haskins & Gregan. She wanted to meet me, so I took some vacation time and flew down for the interview.

Jackie told me about how she started the Houston branch of an Arkansas law firm several years earlier, when the firm's founder, John Haskins, retired. The existing version of the firm consisted of only Jackie, an associate, and their staff. She desperately needed another associate.

Jackie was charming, and in her own way, reminded me of my grandmother: warm and welcoming. She also expressed a desire to teach the medical aspects of the cases, so long as I was willing to put in the crazy hours (and I was).

Working crazy hours was easy—that had always been my life. I accepted the offer on the spot. I had shoveled snow for the last time. Marysue and I loaded up the three kids and moved back to where I was always meant to be: Texas!

Pennsylvania

A hard, half-inflated mattress.
A cold, lonely night.
Clients demanding hours,
Don't understand the fight.

Friends try easing lonely,
And they invite me out for beers.
But that does not fill the empty,
It just postpones the fears.

This cannot be my calling,
This cannot be my end.
This place is cold and lonely,
But to the enemy, I won't bend.

Texas calls me home again,
And home again I'll go.
I cannot wait to leave this place,
Cold, lonely—full of snow.

The Lone Star Lawyer

T he associate's position with Haskins & Gregan gave me the opportunity to represent victims of medical malpractice and nursing home neglect. I learned enough medicine (pulling many all-nighters in our medical library) to have some success in the courtrooms against doctors and nurses who had been inattentive, or worse. I was shocked at the lack of care that I was learning exists!

I sued doctors, who were trained to take care of our most vulnerable—newborns—but simply ignored the clear warning signs of fetal distress, leading to a lifetime of devastation for the child and the family. Most of these cerebral palsy cases could have been avoided if only these physicians had done their jobs and paid attention.

I worked with Patti Artavia, a funny and smart paralegal, who helped prepare my cases for trial. I learned as much from her as I did from Jackie, if not more.

Our investigative staff needed another investigator. Jackie's husband, Kevin, and her son Matt were simply not interested in doing the work anymore. My brother, Reagan, had been complaining about the auto parts retail industry for years. Pep Boys was just not fulfilling for him anymore. Perhaps he would take the job. Reagan jumped at the chance to change careers.

Within two years, the firm changed names: Haskins, Gregan & Kelly. My name was on the door! I'd "made it."

I witnessed insurance companies for these health care providers circle ranks, and threaten expert witnesses that if they testified for an injured person that their own insurance would be terminated. This obvious witness tampering was apparently just par for the course. Our courts would not intervene, even when we presented clear evidence of it. How were we ever going to beat this?

Then came the "tort reform" legislative session of 2003 in Texas. The playing field would be tilted against injured Texans even more. Even if we were successful in court, there would be arbitrary "one-size-fits-all" caps on damages.

That Texas Legislature passed bills that further protected these doctors. I could not understand the level of hypocrisy in the bill, but I realized that speaking out for my clients would fall on deaf ears: people would simply view me exactly as my entire profession had been labeled: a "greedy trial lawyer." Now, no one who actually has the information to expose the corruption of the system could speak without confronting that challenge. I soon realized that these lawmakers, and the insurance companies behind them were simultaneously evil, but brilliant.

What about the Constitution?!

"In Suits at common law, where the value in controversy shall exceed twenty dollars, the right of trial by jury shall be preserved, and no fact tried by a jury, shall be otherwise re-examined in any Court of the United States, than according to the rules of the common law."

7th Amendment to the U.S. Constitution

How was it possible that "The right of trial by jury shall be preserved," but if the jury awards an amount above the caps, that jury's verdict is reduced? Justice was not to be served. The "right to trial by jury" was not being preserved, but rather undermined. The deterrent effect of our jury system was thwarted. So, what was I fighting for as a Marine? What is the point of fallen heroes if we just give away our rights? I had thought that these were the rights we all agreed were worth dying for!

These were the very rights that people before me fought so hard and died for.

The 7th Amendment promises that "no fact tried by a jury, shall be otherwise re-examined in any Court of the United States," so legislators simply took it out of the court and stripped the jury of its power. They completely ignored the preservation language. *Why would they do that?*

Legislators who pushed for this "tort reform" talked about "frivolous" lawsuits but always failed to name one. They conveniently "forgot" that there were already laws in place to punish those who bring such suits.

Actually, they didn't *forget* at all. They just wholly fail to mention it.

They dub my brothers and sisters who would stand up for the injured as *"Greedy Trial Lawyers,"* but that moniker flies in the face of economics. The law of economics, on its face, prevents a plaintiff's attorney from taking on a case that has little chance of success.

This is obvious when you consider that the Trial Lawyer will invest his own money and time into the case, and is ONLY ever paid if they win. What a foolish business model to begin with: those who may be held accountable after that risk is assumed want to convince the public that these well-educated professionals are so illogical as to take these enormous risks on *frivolous* cases?! Though the truth is staring us straight in the face, the facts seem to be ignored, as name-calling is far more attractive to the general public.

As a partner at Haskins, Gregan & Kelly, I was proud of the work we did for so many victims of medical neglect and nursing home abuse, especially in light of the deck that had been stacked against us. We knew that these doctor and nurse defendants were not as saintly as their titles suggested. I was too proud to hold them to account. I completely forget that God put me there.

Despite the public opinion about trial lawyers, our little firm was doing fairly well for what it was. As a partner at the firm, I had finally found my footing and had reached a point where I felt comfortable enough, at long last, to build our family a home. It was a large custom home on an acre and a half of land in a beautiful, gated community. We had designed our "dream," and I finally felt as though I had "arrived." I actually referred to this house as the one I built to die in. I could never have known how that dream would become a nightmare.

Marysue and the kids were oblivious to the struggles of my work, and what the work was doing in my head. While I was finally in a position to "provide" at a level I had always wanted, the weight of being the "bread-winner" was amplified by the fact that my wife's aging parents had moved in with us (they actually helped with the purchase of the home, and my need to overcome that contribution weighed on me daily). Life was good, but the pressure to provide more, and more, were building.

While things looked good from the outside, there was an under-current running through our paradise. Some of the neighbors were doctors, CEOs, and business owners. There was toxic talk and energy in the air. While we did make friends with some of the neighbors. Others felt that the guy who notoriously sued doctors for a living simply didn't fit in. They looked upon me with disdain. This affected my kids: I recall Meghan coming home one day from school and innocently asking me, *"Daddy, why do you hate doctors?"*

"I don't, sweetheart," I replied, having to explain my stance in a way that my grade school daughter could comprehend. *"I simply think that they should be held accountable when they do wrong—just like everybody else. Don't you?"*

In an opinion piece, I wrote in 2002 urging voters to avoid the mistakes we were making by changing the laws in Texas before we actually passed them. The voice of the Trial Lawyer fell on deaf ears. But, as Texans, we pass them anyway at the urging of our legislators (who had to sneak in a change to our Texas Constitution, eviscerating the "open courts" provision to that founding document, in order to make it happen).

Those laws that tilted the scales even further away from justice for injured people took their toll on both my partner and on me—as if the scales weren't already tilted enough!

In the wake of the destruction of our legal protections, Jackie started to drink—a lot. It was clear that the stress for her was starting to overtake her, as she began to come to work in gym clothes. She would claim that she was "working out," which explained why she was never without her water bottle. I was impressed with her dedication until Patti alerted me that wasn't water in that bottle.

Jackie was not alone in her effort to escape the pain caused by these laws that blocked our efforts to help innocent children and defenseless elderly abuse victims. A martini at lunch turned into two, or three…or even four. This became our team's routine to ease the stress.

Sitting at The Fox and Hound one afternoon in 2004, Jackie and I were drinking our lunch, as usual, when a female associate joined us. She had become a regular, too. Feeling way too intoxicated on what was way less alcohol than normal, I found myself entangled with my associate back at the office, where we were nearly caught in the act on the firm's conference table in what should have been a far more embarrassing situation than it ended up being.

I knew then that things had gone too far and that it had to end. The next day, I offered to resign. Jackie was disappointed but asked me not to leave. So, I stayed. And having already crossed the line, the associate and I continued with our affair.

My reckless behavior, between days in the bar and office rendezvous, only worsened. It wasn't long before the drinking caused me to seriously consider my reality (and mortality) as I continued to veer ever closer to impending doom.

Driving home from the Fox and Hound after too many drinks led to more than a couple of close calls with the concrete median on Beltway 8 as I drove home. On one such occasion, I was determined to see my little girl cheer for her team at Fort Bend Baptist Academy (a private school I couldn't really afford). I somehow managed to show up in the stands. My state of intoxication, however, made me far from welcome. My loud, obnoxious rooting and hollering caused such an unacceptable display that Marysue informed me that I had embarrassed my daughter (and the entire family)—and that they never wanted me to come to another game.

These moments of stupidity, together with too many hours that I will never remember, helped me to determine that I didn't want to die in a drunken car crash, or continue to bring shame on my children. That escapism was not worth my life. My life was worth living—even if not for me.

I was starting to see how far I had fallen and became determined to re-shape my life. My boys started taking Karate at a local Karate dojo. I decided to join them and purchased my first *gi*, or karate uniform. Zen-Do Kai Karate became my anti-drug and I loved it.

This situation was perfect, my senseis (instructors), Shawn and Sean, quickly became some of my closest friends. As it turned out, Shawn's fiancée, Heidi, was an attorney who was unhappy at her current firm, which made her a perfect new hire to come work with me and Jackie.

Our friendships blossomed from there, and there was rarely a weekend that we didn't spend together. Heidi would frequently ask me "what are we doing this weekend," as if getting together was a foregone conclusion. The questions were really just "Where?" and "When?" We all showed up.

I practically lived at the dojo when I wasn't at the office. While it was a great escape from the stress (and the booze), it soon became apparent that this anti-drug, too, was widening the rift in my marriage. Marysue and I rarely went to bed at the same time, and intimacy simply wasn't.

She knew about most of my affairs, and an intimate relationship with her cheating husband was, understandably, not at the forefront of her mind. We were both becoming very alone. Once her source of love and companionship, I was now the person she came to when she wanted to go to the salon or to buy Meghan a new purse—if she came to me at all.

I was at least successful in my karate training. With that training, my excessive drinking came to an end. I was moving through the ranks with my boys and was enjoying this special time together with them. I was watching them grow and progress into young men and I could not have been more proud.

Shawn was the consummate martial artist. He had been training since he was 9 years old. He had tremendous talent and was great with kids. He was short in stature, with a shaved head. He was a typical jokester, keeping a sense of humor about everything he did. Karate, however, was his passion.

Sean, on the other hand, was quiet. He was a little larger than Shawn and prided himself not on speed and agility (like his counterpart), but on being highly technical in the art. He was the perfect complement to Shawn.

These two took their belt tests together for every belt since they were red belts. They complemented each other perfectly, and they were best friends.

Back at the office, however, Jackie's downward spiral only worsened. Her trajectory finally came to fruition in a trial in Beaumont. She asked me to go with her, even though I had not been particularly involved in the case up to that point. I watched her as she struggled to comprehend the answers from the witnesses, and as she was unable to form coherent questions on cross-examination. She was as sober as sober got for her at that point, but she was incomprehensible.

I knew that she had literally given everything she had to this profession—her youth, her physical health, and even her mental health. I knew that her prime was over. It scared me.

I was already running the day-to-day functions of the office, given the excessive absences and drunkenness of my partner. She seemed intent on this downward spiral that would surely kill her. *"Is it worth it?"* I wondered. *"Is this a life worth living?"*

Jackie knew that I was disappointed in how she was handling the stress of the career we chose, and the strain of not being able to help people as we once did. It was clear that I had simply become a daily reminder to her of what she was supposed to be (even if I was far less than the perfect image of that ideal).

Eventually, Patti, Heidi, Reagan, and I were the only ones actually performing, and supporting this slowly dying law firm. It was a lot of weight for four people to hold that of ten. Try as we did to save it, we soon realized that we were carrying too much. We had serious discussions about breaking out on our own, but worried about how to survive the economic downturn caused by "tort reform." *How would we be able to help our clients now?*

We also worried about what would happen to our new, young associate, Heidi. She was the latest addition to a firm struggling with the weight of significant expenses and new, restrictive laws that deprived our clients of a true jury verdict (depriving us of the ability to make a living). It was clear that she was going to be let go any day. I worried for her and how she'd make a living, especially because she was about to be married to a karate instructor.

All the parts of my little world, it seemed, were somehow inter-connected. Marysue, the kids, and I looked forward to weekends with our friends, Heidi and Shawn. I did not want to see them hurt by what I knew was likely coming.

I knew that jobs were hard to find for young lawyers, but I had room in my home for Heidi and Shawn to live until they got back on their feet. So I told them that I had them covered when that time finally came. It wasn't going to be too different than our weekends together anyway. I did not expect what came next.

After one of her ever-more-frequent alcohol-infused lunches with Kevin, her husband, Jackie came into my office and closed the door.

Here it comes, I thought, *Will she actually make me fire Heidi?*

"I have decided that we can no longer afford you," Jackie says.

My skin went cold. I couldn't move my body, as the oxygen seemed to have been drained from it. I did not see that coming. After all, I'd been running this firm while she drank and smoked marijuana in her office. How was this firm going to survive without someone sober enough to run it?

"Can you give me a minute to gain my composure?"

"Sure."

For the first time since I was fifteen, I had no job—and no prospects. Not to mention that I had now, for the first time ever, been fired.

Marysue's disdain for me at being fired could not be disguised. It was clear that she had lost all respect for the man she once loved, and it was clear that she was right—to a point.

"Just take any job you can find." She urged. *"A real man supports his family."* Her words cut deeply.

"I'm a trial lawyer!" I demanded, desperately trying to hold on to this identity that I had given myself. *"I'd rather cut grass than work for a defense firm!"*

In the midst of my financial desperation and Marysue's urging, I bit the bullet and actually interviewed with an insurance defense firm. They were a captive counsel firm for Zurich North American. The interview went well, and they expressed interest. I felt the need for a long, hot shower when I walked out. I would truly rather cut grass.

"I can't work for those people," I told Marysue when I returned home. *"I meant it when I said I would rather cut grass."*

But, on the brink of bankruptcy and home foreclosure, with three kids and a wife to support, Marysue was not happy with my response. I was already taking an unemployment check just to feed the family. No one, it seemed, was hiring.

I had actually considered using what little savings we had to buy a Koi Pond building company and just build koi ponds and teach karate. I liked the idea of this simple life (sort of like Mr. Miagi from the Karate Kid), but it was not well received at home.

This is what I have become?

Good lawyers don't live like this, do they?

Texas Justice

Justice seems so far away.
I tell those injured every day.
Texas voters just don't know
How far insurance lobby's go...

To cheat, lie and conceal their aim:
To treat your loss of life—a game.
They dubbed us "greedy" who dared to fight—
And do not care what's wrong or right.

You believe what we know is false,
But it leaves so many at a loss.
That could be you—you don't believe
It must be a trick up my long sleeve.

This baby only wants a chance,
Not to run, or play or dance.
That was taken on her birthday.
But those who did it will not pay.

You capped those losses with your vote.
Now they walk in here and gloat.

They know most of you will not believe,
So here they are: you to deceive.

If she is lucky she may get a share
Enough to pay her doctors care.
Her loss of innocence and life:
Not their problem. Not their strife.

The truth is that they skewed the laws.
Insurance money is the cause.
You believe that justice will cost you care,
But of that lie, you must beware.

Our leaders told you doctors came.
Of course, they did—now we are lame.
"More doctors", they decried, as laws were passed.
But do we want those—last in class.

Accountability—they escaped
But our people they have raped.
The flood that fled the other states,
Came where insurers and lawmakers mate.

The laws we passed brought more malpractice.
Still doctors cry: "You must protect us."
The insurance lobby knows their craft.
Texans, they've given you the shaft!

Don't believe me—It won't matter.
Until your tears on my desk splatter,
As I explain you have no case.

TEXAS JUSTICE

Then you'll finally see a trace

Of the evil lies that you have bought—
Too late: in that web you are caught.
You'll hate **me** *now that I've made clear*
What up to now, you refused to hear.

But what if you had heard before?
Would you then storm out my door?
Or would you see this greedy soul
As one with justice as his goal?

Texas Capital from the TTLA Rooftop

Who Moved My Cheese

I was struggling. My family watched it. My kids watched it. I was desperate. I was also ashamed. I had no job, and I really didn't have any prospects to even offer a sense of hope to my family of recovery from my undoing. It was difficult to find the motivation to wake up in the morning with no job to go to, so I sent resumes from my home office hoping each time I hit "return" that the bad luck streak I had been on would find its end.

I had never met Steve Davis or JD Davis, both of the Davis & Davis Law Firm in Houston, before I became jobless. Though they shared the same name (and the same desk), these men are not actually brothers (Well, they are in Christ). They responded to one of my resumes and invited me to meet with them.

When I went to their office to meet with them, the Davis' did not have a job for me. They simply wanted to help me. The heart of a trial lawyer, after all, is to help others, and these men were true trial lawyers with big, open hearts. I didn't even know how they could have known what I needed—aside from a job.

They introduced me to a children's book that I'd never read, entitled *Who Moved My Cheese*. It was an appropriate choice for changing my troubled mindset, as my "cheese" had clearly been moved. Now, where did it go? That was the question!

Understanding that watching me in my current, desperate situation was probably not the healthiest environment for my children, the Davis' offered to let me use a desk and an empty office in their suite while I searched for something more permanent.

This is what I wish people would see when they think of Trial Lawyers instead of what's deliberately portrayed by our adversaries—whom we work to hold accountable in courts of law for their own, true, misdeeds. This is the level of caring that makes us who we are. But, it's also what makes us vulnerable.

I reached out to another trial lawyer, Andy Vickery, of Vickery & Waldner. When I "interviewed" with Andy, he explained the office-sharing arrangement that he had entered with others in the office and showed me the empty office at the end of the hall where he suggested I move in to practice. His partner, Paul Waldner, appropriately referred to that office as "the end of the duodenum."

As I left the office at One Riverway that day and stepped into the parking garage, I stopped and looked toward Heaven, "Okay, God, I hear you. I'll do it."

In that moment, with no prior plan to open my own law firm, The Kelly Law Firm, P.C. was born.

Ready

The room is empty, not a sound.
The air is still, and all around—
The silence, I know, will not last
For the fight is clear, and long since cast.

The strain I wear upon my face,
The fright I've had of this cold place,
Will they see the fear in me?
Or will I hide it so they see...

Something more than what I feel.
Something more akin to steel?
Can I stand with them in the courtroom's well,
Or is this armor just a shell?

Will my words betray my fear?
Or will I speak and make it clear
That justice demands they bend an ear
And send a message all will hear?

The boxes filled with words I've honed
The arguments that I have owned.

But now the other ones arrive—
It seems the enemy is alive.

I count their boxes one by one
The number now has me undone.
What could those boxes be about?
Twice the number...Twice the clout?

I try to calm, relax my wit:
The number won't determine it.
I smile, shake hands. I hate that ass!
I wish these pleasantries would pass.

"Counsel, are you ready to proceed?"
Thank God, the judge—that's all I need.
I hear his words, my hands grow steady—
"Yes, your honor, the Plaintiff's ready."

The Kelly Law Firm

Although I had not planned to open my own law firm, this was the chance to do it right—to focus on cases that moved me, emotionally, and to make a difference in the world.

All I needed now was to find someone to give me a business loan. If I could manage that, I could hire Patti and start to rebuild my team. I honestly didn't think I could do this without her. But the loan was a challenge all to itself, as I didn't have any cases...Oh, and I was broke. I did, however, have one commodity: my reputation for hard work and results.

I hoped that Heidi and Reagan would join me as soon as I could find a way to pay them a salary.

Fortune smiled when a banker friend, who had funded some cases for me while I was working with Jackie, agreed to go out on a limb based on my history with him. He authorized a $60,000 small business loan, which—though not enough to pay me and Patti both—was enough to bring Patti on board if I didn't take a paycheck. So that's what I did. This was my turn to make things right and I knew I could run this firm better than Jackie did!

Cases came. There were a lot of people getting hurt out there by others who just didn't care enough to put safety first. During my first six months of business, a lawyer who was a few years behind me at Dickinson, and who practiced in Washington, DC referred a case to me that would change everything: Jamie Leigh Jones, a young military contractor who had reportedly been gang-raped in Iraq by military contractors, then locked in a shipping container when she had the audacity to report what had happened to her.

The signing of that high-profile case lead to a funding company offering to pay off my existing loan and gave my firm additional funding. The first $1 Million line of credit allowed me to bring Heidi and Reagan over. As the cases got better, we grew. We grew quickly.

The Kelly Law Firm had a great run for a while. We were able to generate a fair amount of business through our individual reputations, through word of mouth, and through the tremendous free press we were getting on the military contractor sexual assault cases.

We created and maintained a professional website. The team grew to eight lawyers and a strong, seasoned legal staff. We even opened a second office, and had a national presence through "of counsel" relationships with firms all over the country. We were really doing great things! Students from local law schools wanted to intern in this law firm I had created—just for experience. I hired several—or I let them work there.

As my firm was growing and progressing, so was my martial arts ability and presence. I became a black belt in karate under Shawn and his Sensei, Robert Gifford, at Safety America. Along with my promotion to black belt, I was asked to take over the operation and ownership of the karate school. This happened within months of opening my firm. It was going to take more time away from home, but I rationalized that I could train *with* the boys in the evenings. I rebranded this Safety America branch location into Lone Star Karate & Self-Defense.

At the firm, the Jamie Leigh Jones case had put us on the map. Jamie and I were interviewed by 20/20's Brian Ross, and featured on that television news program along with other victims of sexual abuse by military contractors.

We were also featured on both the Rachael Maddow Show and on MSNBC. Her story, and our fight for justice, were featured as one of the four cases detailed in the documentary film, *Hot Coffee, the Movie.*

As media hype and controversy around her case heated up, Jamie and I were invited to Washington DC to speak to legislators about the evils of pre-dispute, mandatory, binding, secret, arbitration—especially as it applied to military contractors overseas.

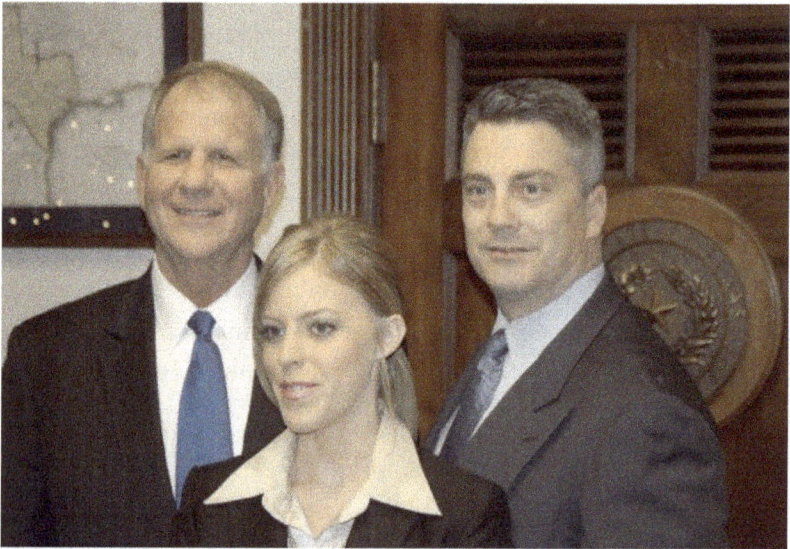

With Rep. Ted Poe and Jamie Leigh Jones

With Sen. Al Franken

Some federal laws were changed. Arbitration was defeated (at least temporarily) in the narrow context of military contractors involved in sexual assault allegations. I took enormous pride in my team's efforts to assist in this corporate giant's arbitration clause being struck down for the first time in its history.

Jon Stewart did a segment referring to legislation around Jamie's case on The Daily Show, entitled "Rape Nuts." That is when my son, Josh actually recognized that his dad was up to something big—when Jon Stewart talked about it.

Presenting on the Fairness in Arbitration Act Bill on Capitol Hill with Jamie Leigh Jones. Sen. Hank Johnson of Georgia in the background.

Local news programs picked us up on numerous occasions. Prospective clients were calling around the clock! Jamie and I were recognized for our efforts by the American Association for Justice, where she was awarded with the *Making a Difference* Award, and where I was invited to speak on the struggles of navigating her case. We were also invited to present her story to law schools, including the University of Texas. The National Employment Lawyers' Association asked us to come and present her story at their annual conference.

I started believing in my own press. Really nice things get written when you're winning. I took it all in and savored all the glory as if it were all according to my own plan. I had started to believe that I did this myself. I, to my shame, had forgotten the One who gave me this chance—my Savior, my God. Jesus, I am sorry.

Jamie Jones is Presented with the Making a Difference Award by the
American Association for Justice

Despite the improvements in my public image, my life at home was falling apart. Between karate and a crazy travel and work schedule, I was rarely home; and when I was home, there was only arguing. Marysue had lost all trust in me, and rightfully so. I had proven too many times that my confidence comes from the attention of women. I had taken that attention wherever I could find it, and I was traveling out of town, a lot.

Marysue demanded more of my time, but time was a commodity I simply didn't have. I was struggling in my effort to keep things afloat, and she was not really interested in my work. I couldn't focus on our "parenting methods," or our "time together," when I had a case that demanded that I give every ounce of my being to, all the time. My common response was *"I cannot do that now—Jamie needs me."*

As the case progressed, even more of my attention was demanded. Mysterious things happened during the course of Jamie's case against Halliburton and KBR. One witness mysteriously drove off a road in California to her death. A local court reporter, with whom I had become friends over the years, died in her kitchen with the transcript of the deposition of the alleged rapist still in the process of being transcribed on her computer. There were other mysterious happenings. Coincidence? Perhaps.

At some point, I called a meeting of my firm to discuss the literal risks of taking on the world's largest military contractor. As I sat down at the conference room table, I looked each member of my dedicated team in the eye.

"I don't know exactly what we are up against, or if we're truly in any danger, but if any of you do not want to stay, I understand. I'll write you letters of recommendation and help you find other jobs." I told them. *"I have decided that The Kelly Law Firm will be pursuing justice for Jamie Jones regardless of risk."*

I had decided that *this* cause may have been the very reason for my life. If it costs that, then so be it. My brave team agreed. Not one person left. Courage on my team was evident: This case, and everything it stood for was worth the risk to every one of them. As I reflect on it, I would be credited with the courage, but this team was full of that quality.

While fighting Jamie's case under public scrutiny, I was also involved in a toxic tort chemical case that took an equal amount of time, and far more financial investment from my firm. My financial backers encouraged relationships I would never have been a part of except for that pressure from folks with their hands around the neck of my money bags. I became involved with lawyers who did not have the same client-centered focus that I had seen in other trial lawyers. These lawyers, it turned out, were not, normally, lawyers for people (Trial Lawyers). They were, I would learn, in it only for the money.

Collectively, we borrowed over $30 Million to fund the litigation against BNSF Railroad for dumping creosote all over the town of Somerville, Texas. While the lawyers who brought us into the case were not my type of people, the cause was just. Creosote, the material used to coat railroad ties, had been dumped in the lake, buried in the ground and burned, so that it permeated the air—all over this pretty little Texas town, for decades. People in Somerville, Texas were being born with birth defects at an alarming rate, and dying in their early 50s of cancers rarely seen in people that young. But, they didn't realize what was killing and maiming them.

I didn't actually try these cases, because of my focus on the Jones case, but I had partnered with lawyers that I trusted. The lawyers who encouraged my involvement had me convinced that they would succeed and change my financial situation for the better. I decided that this one had to be just a business deal, given my other commitments. So I kept my focus on Jamie. That's how I had to view it.

My line of credit, however, had gotten out of hand due to the funding of the Somerville litigation. It seemed that my firm was now on very shaky financial ground. I borrowed millions of dollars to support the Somerville litigation as well as the other cases I was involved in. I had become completely dependent on the lenders. What I didn't know about those borrowed funds was that they were really part of a Ponzi scheme disguised as a lending institution.

The trial team lost the first of the Somerville cases. I didn't have time to take that on, personally. So I withdrew and cut my substantial losses before they got worse. If I was to have any chance of saving my law firm, I had to focus. I was now personally in debt to the Ponzi scheme lenders for over $12 Million. I was, once again, at the end of my professional rope... unless I could bring justice to Jamie Leigh Jones.

I knew that Jamie's case was righteous and worth my sacrifice, and I had put all of my trust and hope in my belief that the jury would eventually see the truth and do the "right thing," if I could just get it to a trial.

There was an arbitration provision in Jamie's employment contract, and the military contractor wanted to compel her case into binding, secret, un-appealable arbitration (where cases go to die). Arbitration is one-sided, secret, and full of reasons why the "little guy" will never have a fair shot against a large corporate entity, so I fought arbitration at all costs.

Against all odds, we beat Halliburton's forced, secret, pre-dispute, binding arbitration provision at the trial court level.

We even held on to that ruling at The Fifth Circuit Court of Appeals. We were going to get a trial!

The Spark

She wanted only to be free
From lecherous men at home.
She took with her the dream she had,
That she was not alone.

She believed she was a part,
Of a team of righteous men.
But that belief would lead her down
A road others had been.

Just a girl she signed away
Her right to jury trial.
Not known to her but to the men...
She'd face harm in a while.

She tried to make some friends you see
On that fateful summer day.
They drugged her, then each took their turn,
As if some sort of play.

They drugged her as they passed a drink
She took in naïve trust.

They watched her consciousness recede
And then appeased their lust.

Lust for sex, or power—so
It really matters not.
It only mattered to them then
That they knew they'd not be caught.

They never thought they'd pay a price:
They never had before.
She was not treated as her friend,
They raped her, and what's more:

They tore her body as they laughed
And really didn't care.
They knew her story'd never pass,
So her body they would share.

They'd never paid a price before
For doing evil things.
Military contractors
Ignored these evil rings.

Profits depended first, you see
Upon the public's view.
It serves their greedy means therefore
For justice to be skewed.

They force those suffering before
Who had the nerve to tell
Into secret "resolution"—

115

And, thus: a silent Hell.

Call it quick, quiet, easy—see
Just like the Star Chamber
Arbitration, DRP
Just keep a lid on her!

That's how the royal "nobles"
In England's tyranny of Olde
Kept rule over the lowly serfs,
And history has told...

That the founding fathers of our land
Despised this power, greed, and might.
They chose to have no part in these
So they wrote a Bill of Rights.

Keep the secret in the dark,
Don't let the public see.
But this one chose to be the spark,
We wish we all could be.

Refusing to accept that this
Was "related" to her job,
She took her fight into the courts
And stirred an angry mob.

Her fight was won in courts and then
On appeal and more.
Congress took an interest in
What happened off our shore.

THE SPARK

She changed the law for others too,
Raped, assaulted and harassed.
Because her heart and cause were true,
Better laws were passed.

But her employer still refused
To admit complicity
In the evil that misshaped her body
And stirred this swarm of bees.

So off to trial she had to go
To make them answer for
All the things they did to her
And the women raped before.

As we consider who is right,
Which way those scales should tilt—
I have to ask you, isn't this
Why courtrooms first were built?

They painted her story as
One built on greed and lies.
Their money bought a verdict,
But that's no great surprise.

At least when she lays down at night
Jamie knows the truth:
They had to fight with all their might,
To keep justice from this youth.

The Ranch

Suite 1100 at One Riverway in Houston, Texas was a showpiece of an office. Sitting on the eleventh floor of this sky-rise in Houston's Galleria area, our office space housed five law firms that worked together in a collaborative effort as "Justice Seekers." The firm logos were etched into the glass doors at the front of our suite. It had the look and feel of a distinguished, successful law firm. The tenants in the suite often worked out the details of our cases in the office space's mock courtroom (a sign of our self-perceived importance), preparing our clients and ourselves for the battle that is a trial.

These brother and sister Trial Lawyers introduced me to the methods of trial presentation taught at the Trial Lawyers' College. Most notably, my close friends Ron Estefan and Andy Rubenstein taught me how to use these methods to connect on a deeper level with my clients, and to "walk a mile in their shoes."

I first applied to the Trial Lawyers' College in 2007, and was disappointed when I was not accepted into that class. I would try and fail again in 2008 despite assurances that I'd be accepted. But, I was privileged to work with masters of the technique in our suite for those years before I finally got the call to attend the 3-week course in Dubois, Wyoming in July of 2009. In addition to my office mates, Ron and Andy, I was introduced to one of my mentors and heroes in the practice of law, S. Rafe Foreman. Rafe practiced with his dear friend and fellow TLC sister, Susan Hutchison in Flower Mound, Texas. I joked—half-joked—that these two were what I hoped my partner, Heidi, and I would be like "when we grew up." They were, simply, magical together.

In addition to the trial techniques that I knew I wanted to learn, I was also learning that in order to "walk in my client's hide," I first had to know myself at a level much deeper than I had allowed up to this point, and probably better than I really wanted to, at that time, given my behavior with women. The methodology for both of these lofty goals was a process known as psychodrama—the re-enacting of events so as to stir emotion, memory, and creativity.

The first week of Trial Lawyers' College was dedicated to personal, inward-looking, psycho-dramatic work. It was work that had to be done "on the horse." I showed up open to the process, due in large part to the preparatory work that my friends had done with me. I was awakened to the fact that my trauma was coming from many aspects of my life: second-hand stress from cases I had been trying to help on; a marriage that was failing, miserably; my own rejection of God's call on my life—just to name the top three demons I had to deal with. There were certainly others. AJ's betrayal was not on the surface, but it was not very far below.

I learned to open up more with my clients, and that it was okay to share with them how their stories affected me—after all, these same stories would be told to a jury at some point, right? How these stories impact the listener is the heart of our craft.

I was ready to change and to face the world with this newfound openness and honesty I had been shown. But when I got back home, despite doing my best to listen and hear more about her concerns about our marriage, the kids, the house, the mortgage, the high utility costs, Meghan's dates... I chose not to discuss my feelings. I told Marysue that I enjoyed the class and that I was glad to be back home. I exercised escapism and ultimately fell back into my old routines.

Trial Lawyers College Graduation: July, 2009

The Greedy Plaintiff

You hate my "greedy" clients, but I hope that you will hear
That when I see the devastation to those that you hold dear
I tell them how you feel and that their damages are naught
Because it doesn't matter right or wrong—as once we all were taught.

They tell me, one and all, how their case is not "the same."
For they have never been involved in this litigation game.
Their damages are real, they urge, and their cause of action just—
Unlike my "other" clients—who just chase their money lust.

As they unfold to me their story, "I am different" they all claim
Though every time I hear it, it is hauntingly the same.
They voted for the laws now used to minimize their right
In favor of a corporate interest—so it could flex its might.

Those with money bought the power and the politicians too.
Justice cost them money, and the wealthy clearly knew
That protecting ill-gained profits means to take—but not to pay
Even when they harmed us all—if blame they could defray.

Now armed with only me, and the system that they scorned
These "different" injured people see the lies that they adorned.

They now see how the wealthy, corporate entities deceived—
Far from paying for the harm they caused, they now will be relieved.

They bought the laws our Founders meant to equalize us all.
It didn't take a battle—not one of them did fall.
They simply used their money, power, might mixed in with greed.
To convince you all that these protective laws were not a need.

Justice will not find its way to help your loved ones now.
You scorned and mocked me all those years, as I tried to tell you how.
I'm sorry, truly, that the corporate lies that you have bought.
Now find you broken, bankrupt, in the web in which you're caught.

I used to think it justice when those who voted out their right
Were forced to fight an enemy with money, and its might.
But now I just feel sorry—for the people didn't know,
And they go home defeated. But the bottom lines still grow.

So heed my tearful warning, all of you who might be harmed.
If you by corporation's greed have been so wholly charmed.
Do you really think they'll help you when they cause you death or pain,
Or will your pleas for justice, like the "others," meet disdain?

If you think that you are different than those they've harmed before:
Those who needed help to cross the threshold of my door,
I hope you never have to learn the hard and awful truth:
That justice for so many is a dream that died with youth.

But the dream was not allowed a peaceful way to die
My brother, sister warriors have held this battle cry.
You do not listen, do not care, until it strikes your home

And once it does its far too late—now with us you will roam.

But labeled, "Greedy Plaintiff" with your "frivolous lawsuit,"
No one cares to hear about your aimless, "lottery" pursuit.
The Trial Lawyer that you hired will do his best to sway,
But it would have been much better if you'd listened yesterday.

At The Trial Lawyers College in July 2009

Back to Business

We were on our way to the U.S. Supreme Court in the *Jones* case on the landmark issue of the enforceability of pre-dispute, binding arbitration provisions. It would affect the outcome for sexual assault victims from this point forward. It could actually stem the tide of these assaults by holding corporations who permit these atrocities accountable. I was also going to get to argue a case at the United States Supreme Court!

Before the case was heard at the Supreme Court, we gained considerable ground on legislation pending in Congress. Enough ground that the company withdrew its Supreme Court appeal. Though disappointed that I didn't get to argue in the highest court of our land, I was relieved that I had won that issue. Against all odds, we were going to get a trial of Jamie's case in federal district court! There were no further hurdles to clear.

We had succeeded as the pointy end of a spear that would bring justice to so many other women who were waiting for this one to pierce the armor. We had done it!

That victory alone filled me with pride greater than I had ever experienced. I find myself searching the internet for the next, best story about "my victory." I create scrapbooks of these accolades and bask in the glow of my victory. But pride, as you know, is a dangerous thing, and blinded by its allure, I had never been weaker.

Robbye Delle Bryan, a student at the South Texas College of Law, came to work for me when her friend, a classmate of hers who worked for me as an intern, Marissa Giovenco, told her that she'd enjoy interning at The Kelly Law Firm and that I was the type of boss who'd be understanding when she had to go home to visit with her dying grandfather who had just been diagnosed with terminal cancer. Of course, I would be understanding. What kind of plaintiff's lawyer would I be if I didn't care enough about people to understand the loss of a family member?

As I frequently do when bringing on a new employee, I checked out Robbye's social media posts on Facebook. Typical, fun-loving, law school stuff. She had family from West Texas. Like my East-Texas roots, they were country to the core. I liked that. She was red-headed when I met her, but had been intermittently blond, various shades of brunette, and even rainbow-colored, since then. Her eyes were bright, blue (or green—depending on the light) that complimented her light freckles, earned during her childhood summers in the sun. Her disposition was bubbly, gentle, and kind. I didn't realize at first the pain she was hiding behind her pretty smile and funny (but awkward) jokes.

Robbye had her eye set on becoming a prosecutor or going into the FBI after graduation. Laudable goals, to be sure. Since my career started with similar goals, I took it on as my personal mission to educate her—to change her mind. That well-intended goal led to close talks and discussions about the practice of law as a personal injury plaintiff's trial lawyer, and to quite a bit of one-on-one time, which I didn't mind. Robbye was fun to be around.

As I endeavored to fill the role as her mentor, Robbye and I bonded and became close friends. Conversations about legal strategy soon turned into more intimate discussions about family and personal topics. Neither of us wanted or expected more to come from our friendship—at first. We worked in close proximity whenever we could and appeared to be attracted to each other. She brushed by me as we would pass one another. It would be wrong, we agreed. I would catch a glimpse of her as I stood over her computer station. It would be cliché, we agreed again. Robbye made it clear that she did not want to be "the other woman."

I felt a connection to Robbye on one specific occasion, as she and Marissa stood behind me editing a legal brief. Just as I started to type, Robbye would say aloud the *exact* phrase I was about to use. It seemed a little funny at the time, but the connection was obvious—we were completely in tune with one another.

Then, on another occasion, I casually brushed against her while we were editing a document on her computer. I felt a chill run down my spine when we touched. I would later learn that she felt it, too. There was an undeniable electricity between us.

The connection was just too strong to be denied.

Every time I walked near her I looked for an excuse to stop and talk to her.

It would be destructive, and neither of us wanted that, still, we agreed. We found excuses to touch. I had done enough destruction. We tried to ignore the feelings of mutual attraction we shared for one another. Those feelings grew anyway. I started to work late. So did she.

Robbye was cute. We both tried to ignore our feelings. A million reasons raced through my mind trying to convince me to leave her alone and just let it be:

I'm too old for her—I tried to convince myself.

I am married.

She is dating other guys.

I tried to focus on work.

I walked away from her.

But I could not stop thinking about her. Things at home were not good, and when I was with Robbye I felt wanted and respected. Respect wasn't something I'd felt at home for quite some time.

Robbye was a victim of a prior sexual assault. She was keenly aware of the emotions that such a violent act evoked, and provided keen insight into how to work with Jaime. She was sensitive and intuitive. I asked her to help me with the case. She was masterful—though still a law school student.

I wanted her. At first, I tried to tell myself that the momentary pleasure would not be worth the damage (again), and I tried to move past it. Still, I wanted her.

My heart was set on her, but I convinced myself that she must remain, despite my desires, just that cute intern from South Texas College of Law that I fantasized about.

I admitted these feelings to almost no one. The exception to that rule was my close friend, Ron Estefan. Ron had been my friend since the inception of the Kelly Law Firm, running his own solo practice out of the same suite, and teaching me the methods of trial skills I worked on at the Trial Lawyers' College. Ron and I actually tried a case using the methods before I was ever accepted to the Trial Lawyers' College. I trusted Ron with this knowledge because it had to get out to someone, and he had become a confidant.

After work one evening, Robbye and I were talking and she expressed to me a view of herself that was not flattering. She was having a difficult time. I had to leave the office but asked for her cell phone number. We talked for most of my hour-long drive home, and I desperately wanted to be there for her. I wanted to help her. Mostly, I wanted her to know how truly beautiful she was inside and out, to me. I recall telling her, *"I just wish you could see yourself through my eyes."*

Working together as closely as we did, particularly when dealing with the raw and often troubling emotions from our cases, especially Jamie Leigh Jones's rape case, Robbye and I eventually came to admit that our feelings for each other had turned romantic and that we had felt the pull from very early on. Nevertheless, we agreed to refrain from acting on those emotions in any physical way. That agreement seemed only to fan the flames. I was truly, madly, and deeply in love with her. It didn't take long before our agreement to keep ourselves apart hit its end.

While Robbye was celebrating a friend's birthday at dinner near the office, I called her just to chat and catch up. She told me where she was, and since she was nearby, she asked if I wanted to just swing by. I did. Robbye met me at my truck and jumped in. The emotion of the day, the beautiful dress she was wearing, the way she was looking at me. I leaned in…

We kissed. *Finally!*

The secret between us was officially on, and the emotional tinder box was open.

The following week, we attended a settlement hearing in district court in Houston for the final resolution of a settlement on behalf of a child who had suffered a birth injury. The trip was purely professional and intended for her education. Despite that barrier having been shattered, I did not plan on more. On the way home, however, we couldn't avoid a discussion about our feelings for one another. I pulled over to continue the discussion out of the earshot of our office mates. It was there, on the side of the road in Memorial Park on that ride home from the Harris County District Courthouse that I told her, for the first time, that I loved her. Then, again, we kissed.

I never wanted that kiss to end.

My partner, Heidi, who had been on maternity leave returned to the office a few weeks later. Her uncanny ability to read me, born of our close friendship, betrayed my "well-kept" secret about Robbye. As I walked by Heidi's office and poked my head in to say hello, she was drumming her fingers along her desk as if I was in trouble.

Who owns this firm, anyway?

"Everything okay?" I asked, knowing full well that something was wrong, and not really wanting her answer.

"*Really?! The intern!*" She scoffed, looking at me as if I had truly lost my mind.

When I told Robbye about the exchange with Heidi, she immediately resigned from her position at the firm. We continued to see each other, but we decided that it should not happen at the office—especially if we were going to keep our relationship discreet.

My focus promptly turned back to the one area in my life where I had clarity in my focus—the *Jones* case.

Kellogg, Brown & Root, one of the largest government military contractors, which I sued in the case, owned one of the sky-rise buildings in downtown Houston. As if by coincidence, also housed in that building was the local office of the federal Internal Revenue Service. The last clear sign that I was fighting an enemy with which I could not compete came exactly 30 days before opening statements were scheduled in *Jones*. I had never undergone a tax audit before (and I have never been audited since)—and I do not believe in coincidence. But on that May afternoon when the IRS tax auditors contacted me, I knew it was intended to distract me from my focus on the most important case of my career to date.

I called my CPA.

"*I cannot focus on an audit right now, Mark. I have a fiduciary duty to Jamie to put her interests ahead of my own. I need you to handle this.*" I tried to ignore the threat.

Speaking with Reporters outside the federal courthouse in Houston, Texas, 2011. Pictured with Jamie Leigh Jones, Kallan Daigle (her husband), and Ron Estefan, my friend and co-counsel.

As Jamie's trial commenced, I stood by Jamie's side, with my friend, Ron Estefan, as my co-counsel. The trial went on for three full weeks—an eternity in Federal Court. Press crews were waiting for us like buzzards over decaying meat every day as we left the courthouse. We believed that we were winning, and we knew our cause was true.

As I delivered the closing argument in the case, I became over-whelmed with emotion. I turned to my friend, Jamie, who I had been "protecting" for almost five years. *"I can no longer protect you,"* I tell her in front of the jury. *"You're in their hands, now."* I then sat down, exhausted, releasing her fate to a federal jury of her peers.

I gambled it all—my reputation, my money, my firm, my future, my children's future, my career on one case that I believed in…

…that I *still* believe in. Jamie's case had to be my redemption.

131

The jury deliberated for 10 hours over the course of two days. We were certain that we had won—we could feel the stress from the defense lawyers pacing the hallways. We had to fight to contain our excitement, to project professionalism.

In the moments when I allowed myself to think about what the verdict would mean to me, I was sure that we had also saved my law firm. I wondered what settlement offer they might make to avoid a large verdict. I imagined that the jury would punish these evil companies and send a loud message—the only way it can. Would I retire? Would I pay off the house and send the wolves to some other door? Would I buy a beach house?

But, in one devastating answer, the jury crushed those dreams. It seemed my entire world was torpedoed with one, unexpected blow that stripped Jamie of justice, ended The Kelly Law Firm and eviscerated my personal goodwill and reputation in the press. They simply didn't believe her story.

I dissected this case many times over after that verdict (and I likely will for the rest of my life). I wrestled with the details of the rulings. I imagined all sorts of untoward happenings behind the scenes.

Of course, something else happened—they sent the IRS into my office, right?

I had put everything I had into that case: my time, my money, my emotion, my reputation, my credibility, my children, my faith, *everything*. I believed that I had to truly "put my money where my mouth is;" and I'd lost. I'd lost *everything*...

More importantly, I'd lost for this courageous woman I had grown to love, Jamie Jones. I took on the responsibility to protect her and achieve justice for her. I had failed her.

I was personally crushed and offended each time Jamie's integrity was challenged in the press—but I was now powerless to respond. I felt the need to protect her "against all enemies," regardless of where they came from. I had dedicated years to protecting her—and in the end, I failed her. Now, I felt powerless to help her, crushed under the weight of this loss and the collapse of my personal life.

Leaving Court during the Jones trial

Was I always inadequate? Probably.

And I had failed my family—repeatedly.

And I had failed Robbye.

And I had failed my law firm.

And I had failed my partner, Heidi.

And I had failed my brother, Reagan.

And I failed my friend and trial partner, Ron.

I didn't wear that failure publicly. I wouldn't. I somehow remained too proud.

I wallowed in my own self-destruction. This was Satan's playground: a defeated man who had become separated from and lost his way back to the Savior.

Like a rendition of a "Reverse Psalm 23," I appeared to have lost everything:

I've left the Lord my shepherd. I am wanting.
I am unable to lie down in green pastures.
I find myself in chaotic waters.
My soul is exhausted.
I walk down paths in the wrong direction.
As I walk through the valley of the shadow of death, I fear every evil for God is not with me.
There is no rod or staff to comfort me.
I go hungry before my enemies.
I have lost the anointing and am desperate for blessing.
Goodness and mercy do not follow me, but I must chase them, every day of my life.
I will not dwell in the house of the Lord forever.[1]

Forever.

After three days of staring aimlessly at an idiot box mounted in front of the leather recliner that I had sunken deeply into in my bedroom, I pry myself out of that leather tomb and crawl to the closet to find my

---

[1] I need to acknowledge the work of Pastor Avery Montgomery and his lovely wife, Zion, both of Celebration Church, Georgetown, Texas for this contribution. It is reprinted here with their blessing.

cold, black Beretta.

Well cared for—like any good Marine's weapon.

I pick it up. I almost caress the cold, metal, barrel, the rough hand grips.

I smell the CLR cleaning fluid on the metal. I feel the slightly oily surface of its protection from rust.

With my left hand, I pull the slide back to lock it in place.

As I release the catch with my right thumb, the slide chambers a hollow-point round with an almost echo. The familiar noise is ominous this time.

I flip the safety upwards with my thumb, exposing the red dot below the safety catch.

Locked and Loaded.

Slowly, I lift the instrument of destruction to my mouth.

Tears well in my eyes. This loss is worth dying for. There is no rush. No one is home. I am, utterly, alone.

This—is the moment where this story began.

Loser

When you've lost in front of everyone
Your life, it seems, has come undone.
Pride, its own ferocious beast,
Took over and it never ceased.

Winning trials and seeking fame,
Seemed all that mattered in this "game,"
Until the time came to pay up,
And none of that could fill my cup.

I hadn't been the man I should,
I hadn't really been that good.
I cheated on my wife – no shame.
Again, I thought it just a game.

My victory would tell my story,
As I walked around in glory.
Nothing else I'd lost would show
I'd simply bask in fortune's glow.

How easily we are deceived,
Until of fortune, we're relieved.

LOSER

Sitting in the stillness now,
I fell so far, and don't know how.

I cannot face my family, friends
I guess this is how it ends.
In shame, disgrace, and all alone,
Unless I could somehow atone.

Perhaps there might be a way,
To lift my head again someday?
That's just a dream, you stupid boozer,
Don't you see, you're just a loser.

Out of The Closet

I had neither showered, nor shaved, since the jury returned its verdict in favor of these military contractors, depriving my dear friend, Jamie, of justice. I smelled of body odor and Scotch. My hair was matted—but short. I was disgusting, even to myself.

I am not sure if I had eaten. If I had, it was only because of the kindness of the woman I was once in love with, who bore me three children. Though we normally didn't get along, she had been more supportive through this loss than I deserved.

I sat in front of a television that merely provided background clatter, protecting me from the haunting silence. I had not actually watched a single show—except the occasional news story about my humiliating defeat. I stayed glued to those stories hoping, dreaming, that the punchline might somehow be different the next time.

I had considered quitting the law on several occasions in the past. I could teach Karate full-time. I found great joy in teaching those kids about self-defense. But, I could not afford my kids' college on a sensei's pay. What pay? I barely paid the overhead at the dojo with the tuition from karate students.

I would have to sell the house. I built it "to die in." It appeared that wouldn't happen. The irony of that phrase was not lost on me.

I wondered if I could start a lawn-care company. That would have been far less emotionally taxing. I recalled my business evaluation of a koi pond construction company. I'm still young enough, I thought.

My in-laws had moved out into a retirement community, this was too much house, anyway.

I was supposed to be one of the good guys!

Wait, I was hated before. Perhaps I deserved this?

I should have stayed in the Corps to defend my name when AJ betrayed me.

How did I put myself in this mess, chasing "justice?" Why had I not learned that justice is just an illusion?!

Though this is where it started, this is also where this book would have ended except that God was there. He never left me, even though I had refused to see Him. But Our Father knew my heart. It is He who showed me, in vivid detail what my children would have found on the floor of that closet if I had finished what Satan had enticed me to do. Leaving my kids with that final image of their father—on the floor, bleeding from the back of what would be left of my head, and holding the instrument of my self-inflicted death was more than I could do to them—and God knew it. While I didn't feel Him that day, He was there. He was holding me, and He was loving me. All while I was too blind to reach for Him.

I imagined their pain. I feared their last memory of me somehow giving them permission to follow in that path when things get too tough in their own lives. They don't have that permission. I would not (and will not) give it to them.

In the end, I could not leave this world that way.

I put the Beretta back in its bag.

Many of my colleagues have sadly made a different choice.

Many of my brother and sister trial lawyers who take on the "secondary stress" of those for whom we fight every single day cannot find a way out of their own closets. Sadly many of my colleagues have not come back from the stress that they suffer. As they held the triggers of their own pistols to their heads, no one convinced them not to pull. They ignored the messages that God sent them. Many ignored Him completely.

I write this book as a plea: Don't pull the trigger! Our careers, and even our clients, are simply *not* worth dying for.

As I crawled out of my closet and returned to the recliner where I had spent the last three days, I was deflated, I was exhausted, and I was overcome with grief.

I sat there waiting for something to happen. My cell phone rang.

"What are you doing, Todd?" It was Jamie.

"Nothing, Jamie. Just sitting here."

"I hear you haven't gone back to work yet?"

"No."

"Don't you think you should?" she asked.

"I don't know if I can," I admitted, defeated.

"You have at least three other women who have been victimized by the same company. Those are just the ones I know of…"

Then came her magic words: *"…They need you."*

At those three words, I got up. I washed my face. I shaved. I went back to the office.

I knew she was right—they did need me. They needed me to protect them in the same manner that I tried to protect Jamie. I knew that they have no chance without someone fighting for them. In that moment, I was all they had.

They needed me to ignore the naysayers in the press who would denigrate Jamie and her attorney.

Todd Kelly and Jamie Leigh Jones 2009

They needed me to spend more borrowed money and they needed to eat up more of my time. They needed me to stand face-to-face with the largest military contractor in the world as if I could outspend them: to stare them down with confidence, while I stood there shrouded in my own terror.

141

They needed me to be what I didn't know if I still had the strength or courage to continue to be: a trial lawyer.

Somehow, I stood. Somehow, I donned my role. Somehow, I helped.

Several of the victims were compensated for the devastation to their bodies, and for the indignities that they suffered overseas. I cannot say more than this because of the confidentiality provisions in their agreements, but I am proud of the work my team did for them.

It turns out, I also needed them.

They thanked me, and moved on. Their lives would be better now. So would mine.

But The Kelly Law Firm, P.C. had taken its final, fatal blow.

Before I closed the doors to my firm for the last time, I returned to "The Ranch" for a graduate course. I had already paid for it, at any rate.

By the time I made the trek back to attend a graduate course at the Trial Lawyers' College at Thunderhead Ranch in Dubois, Wyoming, I knew and had admitted to myself and to Robbye, that I was hopelessly in love with her. We had now been "outed," as our feelings for one another had grown too strong to conceal from anyone in our vicinity. We tried not to go out publicly because I was still married, but it was clear that Robbye had my heart. I was miserable in my marriage at that point, but I knew "right from wrong," and I struggled.

I was chosen as the protagonist in a psychodrama about this raging internal conflict in the "Johnson Barn" at the ranch, directed by Don Clarkson, a master at the craft. Don Clarkson may well be one of the most talented psycho-dramatists alive. Don directed me to dig inward and face the choice that I would inevitably have to make. As he directed, I chose people in the room to play the roles of Robbye, Marysue, and each of my children. Don chose Joey Low, a fellow Marine, to play my conscience. With Joey yelling in my ear about doing the right thing, and the faces of my wife and children looking at me, I had a difficult time looking at Robbye (played by my now dear friend, Lori Gingery).

I made the "right choice" to stay with Marysue initially but was literally in a ball of tears on the floor of the barn because I could not accept losing Robbye. Don directed,

"The wonderful thing about psychodrama is that we get to make every choice to see what works, so get up and choose again."

I got up and made the other choice. Holding tightly to my friend, Lori Gingery, in her auxiliary role as Robbye, I felt the pain of loss, but nothing like I had just felt when I chose to live my life without her. I knew that the loss of Marysue would hurt, as would the loss of respect from my kids that I knew would likely follow. I feared that my children would turn from me, and didn't know how long they would remain that way—or if they would ever accept me back into their lives.

After the psycho-dramatic re-enactment and the work of that session, I knew that there was no painless way out of my situation. I was going to hurt someone, actually several people, and I was definitely going to hurt, too. That much was inevitable. But, there was one choice that I knew I simply could not live with: letting Robbye go. Now, I knew what I must do—as hard as it was going to be.

I would jokingly tell Don many times after that, that he was responsible for my life.

"I don't want that responsibility!" was always Don's reply. Don, you have my gratitude.

The personal drama that surrounds my break-up with Marysue once I returned from the ranch is omitted here so as to preserve the privacy that surrounded the issues between her, myself, and the kids. Suffice it to say that it was extremely painful—for all of us. I had betrayed them and I had betrayed the vows I made to their mother. I felt worthless as a husband, as a father, as a man, as a human.

Heidi, whose children still referred to me as "Uncle Todd," closed the door to my office and turned to speak. Before she could utter a word, I saw the tear form in her right eye and roll down her right cheek. She could not speak as her chin quivered. I had never seen Heidi this way. She was normally so unemotional and guarded.

I got up from behind my desk and met her halfway. I hugged her and let her cry. Her sentiment was kind, but the words she could not form had already hurt me to my core.

"You don't have to say it, Heidi, I understand. Do you have a place to land?"

"Yes," she sobbed.

Heidi had not been paid in several months. She had been holding on, hoping—like me—for a breakthrough that never came. And she was loyal. She had continued to hope that we might pull out a miracle in the end.

"I owe you some money," I said to her. *"I have one last settlement check expected, and you will be paid from that."*

"I know you will do what you can."

Heidi and the others that held on were, eventually, paid in full.

The lawyers and staff that worked at the Kelly Law Firm, P.C. when I made the decision to permanently close the doors were mothers, fathers, husbands, and wives; and most importantly to me, they were my friends. This public closing of The Kelly Law Firm would happen simultaneously with my very public divorce.

The partner is paid last—if at all. That is the true hallmark of the "greedy trial lawyer" you hear so much bad press about. That last check was disbursed. Not one penny of it came home.

I was completely broke. And I was completely broken.

My marriage was over. I could not stay in my home.

My firm was destroyed. I had no job.

Somehow, Robbye still chose to be there for me. She remained my rock. Despite rumors and innuendo that inevitably follow a relationship that starts in adultery—and there were plenty—she remained my best friend and my strength. Funny that some saw her as a "gold-

OUT OF THE CLOSET

digger."

Like my partner and the other employees that once called me "boss," I was searching for work. But who wanted to hire the man who had just so famously lost the biggest case of his life on national television—then crashed a law firm—and a family; and who did it all so publicly?

Robbye had a job with another plaintiff's firm, The Mostyn Law Firm, as a legal brief drafter. She took that job when she passed the bar exam. She couldn't return to the Kelly Law Firm since our feelings for one another had become known to Heidi, and we could not conceal our affection for one another.

Robbye's paycheck paid the rent on several occasions because I simply did not have the money. I could no longer live in the house I had built "to die in," as my soon-to-be ex-wife and my children needed that home. Eventually, it would be sold and the proceeds divided in the divorce.

I didn't want to practice law anymore. It had beaten me. But I didn't have any other transferable skills at my age that could make a dent in the student loan debt that Robbye and I were both strapped with. My kids didn't seem to understand why Daddy couldn't just pay for their student loans (I had always thought I would—and I had told them so).

The obvious place to turn in this situation was to God, but I was too ashamed to do so. I wouldn't do so. I had not yet dropped my foolish pride, despite the trouble it had created for me. I knew that I needed to give this to Him because it was way too big for me. I simply could not get out of my own way.

Eventually, Bruce Phillips, a friend that I met through Ron and a fellow lawyer from the Trial Lawyers' College, returned my call. Bruce worked in the San Antonio office of The Carlson Law Firm, a large plaintiff's firm in Central Texas. I remembered how much he raved about the firm he worked for and knew that it was a larger firm that might just have a spot for me.

He arranged an interview with the firm's owner, Craig Carlson, in Killeen, Texas. Craig, it turned out, is a man of God. Where I relied upon my own talents to run a law firm (and we all saw where that led), Craig had relied upon his faith in God to lead him to make relationships and to deal as his faith commands. The difference in results was stark: he ran one of the largest, most successful firms in the state, if not the country. I, on the other hand, ran my firm to crash and burn in a public, humiliating death. It would take me a while to attribute the different outcomes to the One responsible. Like the prodigal I am, I was still too lost to see it. I had apparently not lived in the devastation I created quite long enough...

The Warrior

The trust she placed in me: complete.
Her life she'd laid down at my feet,
My confidence was more than strong,
I had waited for this case so long.

Then came the time to show the world
That I was the one to help this girl.
But victories had made me weak
I did not know: I'd reached my peak.

We made it public—for all to see.
Pride snuck in—it now owned me.
I'll win this case, and in the press.
The world will see my very best.

The world will see a hero, right?
Perhaps there should have been some fright...
The jury fought ten hours plus.
Certainly, they'd ruled for us?

But they answered the first question "No."
A feeling from deep inside did grow.

It stung a bit, but wasn't done.
Before it left I was the one...

The one who sat alone at home
Thoughts of worthlessness did roam.
Others would not share this strife.
For a while I thought I'd end my life.

What could pull me through this grief?
What could bring me some relief?
That Beretta sat just feet away.
But pain was not all that I'd slay.

Others cared—and I knew it too.
But I didn't want them close, that's true.
Shame had taken o'er my heart.
Then I looked back at the start.

I believed I'd built this story.
That I deserved the fame, the glory.
Arrogance, conceit, and pride.
Were all that I now held inside.

Let it go, I'm just one part
Of a larger tale that is the art.
The art of life, and love, and loss,
That like a ship on waves will toss.

I cannot stop the rolling seas,
Or this self-inflicted pain appease.
So take this pride and foolish shame,

THE WARRIOR

I'm only strong when I am lame.

Now remember who you truly are
Stop trying to be someone's star.
Just love your friends, your kids, your wife
The rest is just your busy strife.

The job you do, it matters, sure.
But it's not you, so do not pour
Your whole life into the voice of twelve,
For if you do, your soul you shelve.

Keep your focus on what counts
Know that when the battle mounts
You'll do your best to make it right.
But sometimes evil wins the fight.

Live to fight another day
Do not throw all you've been away.
Put down the gun, lift up your head.
And choose to go back in—instead.

A warrior does not win each fight,
But continues on with all his might.
A warrior would not walk away
This warrior will not die today.

The Phoenix

T he position that Craig Carlson offered me was a serious blow to my once hyper-inflated ego. I had been a *partner* in two firms with my name on the door. I had recently owned one of them. Actually, I still *owned* it, it was just not open, or viable. I was to start over, as an *"associate"*?

Then there was the issue of pay—at less than half of my base pay when I was running my own firm, (in the months when I was actually paid), and less than I had been paid by other firms even ten years earlier. I was initially insulted at the pay cut—but simultaneously desperate to take it, as I had not seen a paycheck in months. I had no choice but to accept. It was August of 2012.

Despite the blow to my ego and to my self-perceived status, both the position and the pay were welcome changes from running a failing firm and not being paid at all, living on what money Robbye could bring home.

After nearly eleven years as a Marine Officer, I was adorned with not one bit of body ink. There was one close call while out on liberty as a young Lieutenant in Korea after consumption of far too much OB Beer—but Staff Sergeant Grimes, my Staff NCO, kindly carried my limp, drunken body from the tattoo parlor and poured me into a cab to return to base camp. I was always thankful that I didn't get that "artist's" rendition of the Eagle, Globe & Anchor emblazoned on my left arm—or wherever else I may have chosen to put it in my drunken state.

Robbye had several small tattoos, and I had considered getting one, too. Now, I was by myself in Austin, Texas following a successful job interview with Craig Carlson, and didn't really want to drive back to Houston alone. Robbye was away on a girl's weekend trip anyway, so it was just an empty rental waiting there.

I found Diablo Rojo (the tattoo studio across from the University of Texas Campus) on that August day in 2012 when Craig offered me the job. I decided that this was as good a time as any to get tattooed.

My first experience with ink was that the pain, while real, is somewhat symbolic, in and of itself. It hurt to plummet to where I was. This symbol *should* hurt. One of the clients I had helped after Jamie's loss bore a dragon tattoo across her entire back. She once told me that the tattoo symbolized the brutality with which she was brutally raped, and that the pain of getting the ink imprinted on her was somehow therapeutic for her. I finally understood.

The phoenix that now adorns my right shoulder was permanently etched into my skin during a three and a half hour sitting. It was (and is) a symbol and reminder of my own emergence from devastation.

I responded to Robbye's call during a break in the etching by sending her a cell phone picture of the tattoo in progress. She had been worried that I had not called her yet to report on the interview. I wasn't sure if she was happy or disappointed when I showed her what I was doing. She had expected me to be on the drive back to Houston rather than staying in Austin and getting my first ink. Perhaps this was selfish, but I felt that this was something I needed to do—alone.

The tattoo symbolized the re-emergence, not only of me as a professional, but as a man.

More importantly, and though I admittedly did not intend it at the time, it would later come to symbolize (for me) my re-birth as a Christian, and as a forgiven son of God.

I struggled, at first, to regain my identity, to regain my self-respect, my dignity. I was new to Austin and largely unknown to the local bar associations. Robbye came with me, as she was able to work remotely for her employer in Houston, the Mostyn Law Firm, and she helped pay the bills that I couldn't.

As a benefit of my employment, Craig paid my dues to join the Capital Area Trial Lawyers' Association and also renewed my lapsing membership in the Texas Trial Lawyers' Association—I simply could not afford those dues on my own. Craig also paid my way back into the American Association for Justice.

I was, for the first time in my professional history, timid from defeat. I still approached all new acquaintances as if they were judging me. Why wouldn't they be judging? I judged me.

The crash of my law firm was still an open wound into my very being. The place where I had best been able to discuss it was at the Ranch. Those classmates, fellow warriors for justice, provided me with safety to discuss my failures free of judgment. They salved the wound. When my Trial Lawyers' College classmate and close friend—no, brother, Scott Webre, called to check on me and inquired about how I was doing (knowing the intense pain of losing my firm and all that experience entails) my answer set me on a path of appreciation that will take some time to fully realize and appreciate.

"I'm actually pretty good, Scott. I have been paid three times in the last couple of months and I haven't settled a single case yet."

That is the summation of the risks that we take as trial lawyers (when we are not working as salaried associates): I was thrilled to have been paid *just for going to work.* That concept had been lost on me as a firm owner who was only paid after everyone else when the case was resolved.

Yes, there are some lawyers who succeed this way—some who make a lot of money. I tried to be that lawyer, and imagine I will try again. But the unsung heroes are the many more who struggle to make ends meet, and to pay of the student loans that they took out believing that it would all be okay because justice is fair: those who work for justice even when it eludes them and leaves them broke and broken. These are some of my heroes.

After working for a firm lead by faith for a few years, Robbye entered the doors of Celebration Church in Georgetown, Texas while I was in Houston at a trial in November of 2015. She loved the message from the pastor, and called me that day to tell me that we have got to go back. It was a couple of weeks before I heard Pastor Joe Champion preach. It took a couple of years before I felt like I was one of God's children again. But eventually, through prayer, through obedience, and through grace, that phoenix started to mean something new: it is no longer about me. It is about the One who proved that He found me worth dying for.

Grace, that only Jesus can offer, has always been there—I just needed to get out of my own way. This is the most important message that I have for my brothers and sisters who may be reading this. We often become so self-important with our legal (or business) acumen and our plaques on the wall that we forget that it is *all* a gift from our Father, and that we are nothing without Him and without His grace. Alternatively, we become so entrenched in our secondary stress that we forget to rely on Him to carry us through it.

The realization that God is in charge eventually enabled me to stand again: to fight for those less fortunate, and those harmed by the acts of others.

L. Todd Kelly and Craig Carlson 2021

Rise

Lady Justice winks. She winks a lot.
I listened and absorbed this thought.
We speak of justice—hard fought for
At home, and far off of our shore.

The document that guides our art,
Drafted that we not drift apart.
Yet as applied, she isn't blind,
Results are not always so kind.

Peeking out from beneath her shield
As she oversees the field,
She guides the way she thinks she should,
Sometimes that Lady can't see the good.

To protect our treasured way of life,
And honor the sacrifice and strife,
I use the ink within my skin
To remind me I must rise again.

If we're to live as was the dream,
We must be more than what we seem

To raise the causes with which we're charged
Our vision must be now enlarged.

We rise again to fight once more,
That's why we get up off the floor.
For if we fail to rise again,
The Lady will not save good men.

We rise not just because we should,
We rise because we do some good.
We have to struggle, and to fight,
Sometimes with every ounce of might.

Lest we hear our client's cries,
Let's return the blinder o'er her eyes
So when the lady tries to wink,
It's only justice that we think

Should be applied in this, our cause.
For if it's otherwise, let's pause:
"We lost our way along this path,"
Will be this nation's epitaph.

Walking

Unfortunately, when I left Virginia in 2001, I drifted away from my faith, and never really found my way back into church until the end of 2015, three years after joining The Carlson Law Firm.

During that interim, as I mentioned in earlier chapters, I enjoyed some sporadic professional success and notoriety—all of which I attributed to my own "heroic" efforts. That prideful arrogance set me up for the humiliating fall that, while destroying my law firm, probably saved my soul.

Pride, arrogance, and adultery also hurt the relationship that I had hoped my children would have with God, as they now saw their human father for the hypocrite that I am. I had failed as their father and as a servant of God in leading them to Him.

I had been unfaithful to their mother—my then wife, and to my God. More to my shame now, I had not really even tried to be faithful to her. I was simply lost and on a path of self-destruction and spiritual death. I didn't care.

It was Robbye's excited phone call in 2015 telling me about hearing the message from a charismatic pastor at Celebration Church, in Georgetown, Texas that brought me back into the Body of Christ. I was in Houston that weekend, preparing for a trial that was set to start on Monday. My mind was not on spiritual things. But God worked in me through Robbye.

One of the principal people that God employed in my own personal salvation story is Pastor Joe Champion. "Pastor Joe" is about a year older than I am, but infinitely wiser. Along with his wife, Lori, who is co-pastor at Celebration Church in Georgetown, Texas, this man has led an army of Christ-followers to bring hope and salvation to many, including me. His ability to apply Biblical understanding to any situation he faces has been a catalyst that grows Celebration Church from just his family of five in the year 2000 to over 16,000 members today.

Following God's call on his life, Pastor Joe and Lori followed the command "*It is Austin*," whispered simultaneously in their souls while they were physically apart but both serving the Lord. In response, they obediently uprooted their young family from their comfortable home in Baton Rouge, Louisiana to found Celebration Church. This story is miraculous and worthy of more lines than I have given it. It is a story that has shaped my own and placed me in a position to tell it. But, Celebration's is not *my* story to tell—at least not on these pages.

That call from Robbye and my return to the family of God saved my soul. God, through the teaching of Pastor Joe, changed my life and my destination. Pastor Joe's leadership guides me into salvation and a deeper walk with Christ than I have ever before experienced.

Today, I am a student at Celebration Leadership Institute. I am again learning to walk—one step at a time.

Don't get me wrong, it wasn't that I didn't know Christ before I heard Pastor Joe's teaching. It was much worse than that: I absolutely knew Him, but I turned my back on Him. Though I am ashamed of my own actions, I hope that when you read this you will understand that God's grace, alone, is what saves. He saved me from the eternal fate I earned. If He will save me after I turned my back on Him, He will save you, too. Just ask.

And I know today that He was there, in that closet, filling me with the images and words that I needed to stop me from pulling that trigger.

What I now understand is that to Him, I (like you) was worth dying for.

I'm Sorry

"Rest your soul," my Savior cries,
"Just trust yourself"—Satan lies.
The world believes the Devil's tongue
I turn from what I knew, when young.

This name I've built with my hard work.
So Jesus is the man I shirk.
I walk my way and ignore His.
I've made my name, I've honed this biz.

Jesus didn't get me here,
So pass the wine, the booze, the beer.
I got up here on my own accord.
There's no obstacle I can't fjord.

The fall is hard when you fall alone.
He would have caught me if I'd atone.
I didn't ask, my pride was strong.
I had ignored Him for so long.

At the bottom, when I then surveyed,
I realized the price I'd paid.

I'M SORRY

It wasn't property, or fame, or might,
That held the strongest, toughest bite.

It was that I turned upon the One
Who for my sake was so undone.
He bore for me a pain so great,
And I returned with worse than hate.

I ignored my Savior's pleas
So now I come upon my knees,
Forgiveness, grace is all I seek.
I've finally learned that strength is meek.

I come to you with peace and love,
That I know comes from You, above.
My arms stretched high, please hold me, God
It's me, your son, it's just me...Todd.

The Rise

T hings changed working for Craig. Not instantly, but change came. People started to call me again. I had some success with a few cases. Colleagues know me from my profoundly public defeat.

"You actually put your money where your mouth is, didn't you?" becomes an all-too-common compliment.

"Yeah—but I lost it all."

There were always knowing laughs. Not *exactly* funny. But it is better now.

I don't worry about money anymore. Not because I am rich, or even set up for life, financially: I'm neither of those things—far from it. Perhaps one day? For now, Robbye and I are still paying off her exorbitant student loans as well as those I took out for my children to go to college, and we are raising our beautiful daughter, Selby Jewel (named for her great-grandmothers on both sides).

I don't worry about money because I have simply learned that worrying will not make it better. I also don't worry because God has told me not to: He's got this. He has proven that He is there. We began tithing (as commanded) when we didn't know how we could make ends meet. Mathematically, they never could. Yet, they do. I discussed it with Pastor Joe after a Sunday breakfast.

"It's God's math," he tells me. He's right. I quit trying to make sense of

it, and simply accept the gift. He is good.

I now focus my energy on spending time with my family, and in my church. I prefer to spend time learning more about what God has planned for my family and for me, and I want to learn how I can lead others to Christ. These are the things that are most important, and they are the things that too many in our "noble profession" lose sight of as we become beleaguered spokespersons for the injured, forsaken, forgotten, and the damned: those injured by the acts of the reckless and neglectful.

We simply take on the second-hand stress of thousands of clients over time. Eventually, it beats us down until we find ourselves in some version of a closet, with a 9mm pistol in our mouths. This, my friends, is simply not worth dying for.

I didn't stop caring about my clients. I could never do this job if I didn't care about people who are hurt by the carelessness, recklessness, or intent of others. I simply learned to care more. To care about my family more, to care about how I spend my time off more, to care about church more, and most importantly, to care about God more.

I started this book because I care to urge a message: Don't Pull the Trigger. It is simply not Worth Dying For. *You* were. As King David wrote in the actual Psalm 23:

> *The LORD is my shepherd; I shall not want.*
> *He maketh me to lie down in green pastures:*
> *He leadeth me beside the still waters.*
> *He restoreth my soul:*
> *He leadeth me in the paths of righteousness for his name's sake.*
> *Yea, though I walk through the valley of the shadow of death,*
> *I will fear no evil:*
> *for thou art with me; Thy rod and thy staff they comfort me.*
> *Thou preparest a table before me in the presence of mine enemies:*

Thou anointest my head with oil; my cup runneth over.
Surely goodness and mercy shall follow me all the days of my life:
And I will dwell in the house of the LORD forever.

(King James Version)

Forever!

If I had pulled that trigger rather than laying my 9mm pistol back down into the range bag, in 2011, the most important chapters of this book would be blank. Of course, the book would never have actually been written at all. I would never have married the love of my life in front of about 350 friends and family at a rustic venue in Georgetown, Texas in October of 2016. I would never have had the chance to reconcile with Joshua, Meghan, and Matthew—or to continue to do so.

I would not know my little Jewel, Selby—in fact, this little gem would never have even existed.

Robbye, Selby Jewel, and Me in 2020

If I had pulled that Trigger, I could not have gotten up to become the president of The Capital Area Trial Lawyers' Association, which actually embraced me despite my failures.

165

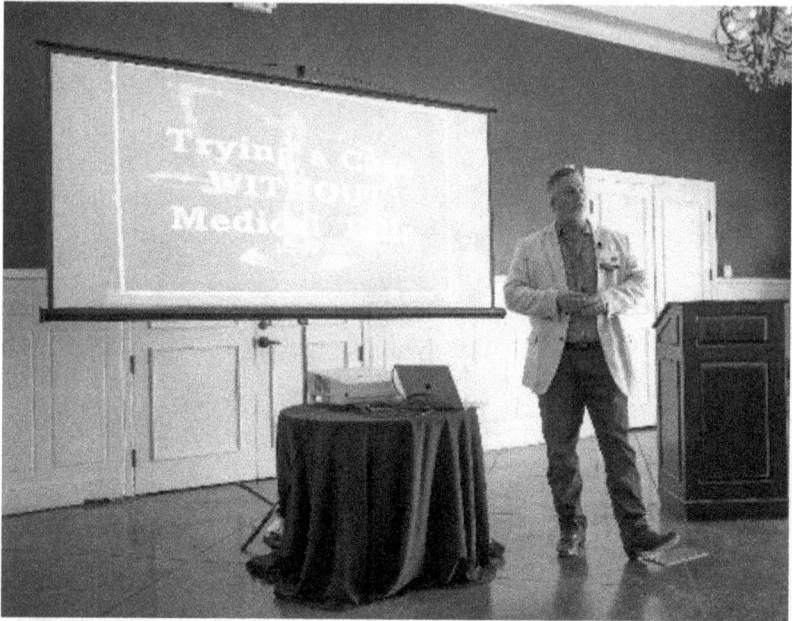

Giving a Presentation to the Capitol Area Trial Lawyers' Association

If I had pulled that trigger, I would never have held office as a vice president in the Texas Trial Lawyers' Association.

Working on Legislative Efforts at Texas Trial Lawyers' Association

If I had pulled that trigger I would not have been inducted into the Texas Lawyers' Hall of Fame in 2013.

Waiting on the Verdict that put me in the Texas Lawyer Hall of Fame

If I had pulled that trigger, I would never have been asked to serve on the central Texas advisory committee for Mothers Against Drunk Driving.

Presenting as Chair of the Advisory Committee for Mothers Against Drunk Driving

If I had pulled that trigger, I would never have seen my name treated with any kind of respect again. I would have simply been a forgotten, failed footnote—another sad trial lawyer. That was not worth dying for!

If I had pulled that trigger, I could not have helped to change the lives that I have been privileged to help over the past decade since that day in the closet.

If I had pulled that trigger, I could not have found my way back to Jesus—the *only one* who has ever found *me* worth dying for.

At Celebration Church in Georgetown, Texas, with Robbye, Joshua, and Selby

During the time since that day in the closet, I have been honored to represent many victims of neglect and recklessness.

I still know the pain that comes from representing these people who share their pain with me; and from fighting an enemy with seemingly endless resources and who disregards the rules of decency, as well as fairness. I know the personal and financial toll that each cause we bring takes. I know the hopelessness that many feel when we do not succeed in finding justice for that client.

And, I know all too well the pain of dealing with a public that maligns and hates us simply for our very existence; to then represent them when they become the injured; and then to have to plead their case to twelve people from that very group who have simply not yet become the victim.

But, I also know there is more. Get up. Find what truly matters in life…and live.

Japanese Kintsukuroi is the art of taking broken pottery and piecing it back together with gold. What was strong and useful became shattered. Then, through love and focus, it became useful again, stronger, and more beautiful. We, like those broken pieces of pottery, can be stronger, more beautiful, and still useful, if we allow God's hands to put us back together again.

It's Not Worth Dying For...

As I consider my role as a counselor and advocate for the clients who need me because of some tragedy that has befallen them and the second-hand stress that accompanies that representation, I cannot help but turn my attention to my Advocate and Counselor, who took on my *entire* burden when He gave His life for me on that cross. He has loved me more deeply and sacrificed more fully to atone for my sin than any amount of stress that I may have the privilege to take on for others of His children. Though I deserve to die for my sin, Jesus did that for me, and will for you, if you simply believe in Him.

I have lost friends who did not heed the plea I make in this book. For one of them (my Karate instructor, Sean, whose pain was more than he could bear, but still not worth dying for)...

Goodbye My Friend

My friend, you never left my heart
I always thought we'd have a start
To reignite our brotherhood—
That friendship was so very good.

I do not know what pain you felt;
What hurtful blow your life had dealt.
I only know it broke you down
And now they'll lay you in the ground.

You were so strong; and funny, too,
My kids and I looked up to you.
We had a falling out, I know,
And so our friendship ceased to grow.

The spot you once held in my heart,
Was always yours to just restart.
I guess I now must say goodbye.
I'll never have that chance to try.

Goodbye my friend, your absence felt
I wish I could have somehow helped.

GOODBYE MY FRIEND

You didn't reach. I didn't know.
The world has lost a good man, though.

Rest in Peace, my friend.

The Reason

As men and women with limited ability to see the ripple effects of what we do, we often do not understand the import. As I sat on the floor of my closet—ready to take my own life because of my failures, I could never have known that the case and the work we had done made any positive difference at all. In fact, it seemed that I had merely fought a losing battle that cost me everything and produced nothing but additional pain for my client and friend, Jamie.

I am a long-time member of the AAJ (American Association for Justice). The AAJ supported my efforts in the litigation during the time that Jamie and I were pursuing justice, and working to change the laws to prohibit mandatory, binding, arbitration provisions in employment contracts. Our position has remained that these provisions are a violation of the 7th Amendment to the United States Constitution, guaranteeing that the right to a civil trial in disputes over $20, shall not be infringed.

On November 4, 2021: I was sitting at an awards ceremony during a conference of the Texas Trial Lawyers' Association in San Antonio, Texas when I received an email from my friend, Vicki Slater, a leader at the American Association for Justice from Mississippi. That email read:

Tears welled up in my eyes as I remembered the jury sending us home in "defeat."

I recalled the look of disbelief in Jamie's eyes.

I felt those days alone in my darkness…

…and I remembered the taste of that Beretta in my mouth.

But, I remembered something else. I remembered *why* I wanted to take on this corporate giant in the first place, and *why* Jamie asked me to: to change the law for the better.

It came over me in waves. After more than a decade; while Jamie would never be compensated for her suffering; my team would never be paid for their dedication, hard work, and personal risk; and while my law firm would not be restored; I now know that we didn't lose at all that day. We had actually done something big, and changed the law for the better! We had done something that made life worth living.·

More than a decade after sitting in that closet in disgrace and shame, ready to take my own life under the weight of that shame and my feelings of worthlessness. The same group of people that I was too ashamed to lift my head to face sent messages to me like these:

This is incredible! Thank you Todd!!

Love,
Cherie Trine

THE POWER WITHIN

Yes. This is a tremendous victory to all involved in this historic step in fighting for justice. Thank you to all

Outstanding work from a lawyer that cares!

Frederick "Rick" I. Hall, III
The Rick Hall Law Firm, LLC
301 Gibson Road
Lexington, S.C. 29072

It's all coming back to me now, Todd.

You stood in when most would have run away, apparently at great personal cost

That's a *real* Warrior. I hope you (and your client) take some solace knowing the brave way you acted will make that road easier for others in the future.

Leo

This is big! You made a difference.

CG

Sent from my iPhone

Congratulations to everyone involved in this
Moosecaller

Regards,

Paul

And today here's Todd Kelly, showing the world how to make a Lotus bloom from the mud of suffering.

Thank you for your hard work, contribution and courage to snatch victory from the jaws of adversity, my friend.

Chris

Todd, I read your article in the Warrior about this case. We don't know each other, but I lost a son to SSRI /Antidepressant induced suicide. It is such a devastating thing to go through and I still hurt from losing him. Your reasoning that kept you here is a gift from God. Grateful you are still with us.

Frederick "Rick" I. Hall, III
The Rick Hall Law Firm, LLC
301 Gibson Road
Lexington, S.C. 29072

It is telling of my brother and sister trial lawyers that these congratulatory accolades are not in response to a large monetary verdict, but about the positive change that was accomplished. These simple messages reveal the true heart of the American Trial Lawyer. Justice and goodness are our True North and money does not change that.

Though we did not know it at the time, God took what Jamie and I had started, and worked through other hands to complete the work in a way we could not have imagined or completed on our own. I post these emails here not for self-gratification (though there is ample joy in receiving them), but rather to show the redeeming power of God's work when we agree to follow Him.

How

You left Your throne—and man, you served,
To wear a crown that I deserved.
We failed to treat You as our King,
And at our hands, You felt death's sting.

You pleaded, cried—tears in Your eyes,
For You knew that You would hear our cries.
Now many turn to You in vain,
And beg You to relieve their pain.

You breathed Your last, the veil was torn,
By Your pure love—a pathway born.
Defeating death, You rose again,
To wash away my very sin.

Thank you Father for all You've done,
For sending us Your only Son,
That when we turn to Him and ask,
Our sins He takes—His promised task.

You carry off my heavy load,
And lead me down that narrow road.

The one You paved for those who will
Answer "yes," and follow still.

You rose to sit at the right of God
And walk where only Angels trod.
The glory Yours, the power, too
Father, we sing praise to You.

We praise You for the fight you've won,
The victory of your slain Son,
But praise also for Amazing Grace,
That removed my sin without a trace.

I don't deserve—and never will,
But as Your promises, You fulfill,
I live again, in freedom now!
Thank you Father—You're the "how."

Dedication

I dedicate this book first and foremost to my Lord, the God of the Universe, who has saved and forgiven me more times than I can count, and so very many more than I deserve. I thank Jesus not only for giving me the strength to tell these stories but for His grace in allowing me to survive them.

I also dedicate this book to my loving wife, Robbye, who has stood by me through the most difficult events mentioned in these pages and has loved me through it all. I thank her for helping me keep the story in chronological order as I found it difficult to recall the timeline of some of the most difficult moments in my life. Mostly, though, thank you for leading me back to Him.

To my children, Joshua, Meghan, Matthew, and Selby—I dedicate this book to you for the sacrifices you've made by having a father whose career choice takes him away so much—both physically and emotionally. I love you all and hope that all who read these words know that you have my heart, my love, my dedication, and my sincerest apologies for the pain I have caused you. My greatest hope for you is that you find your hope in Jesus and that you follow Him to find the joy that it took me so very long to find.

To my mother, Linda, and my father, Jim, who raised me with the courage of conviction and with an example of love for others. I thank you for teaching me the things I needed to know, to eventually stand in the light that I have only recently truly found.

To Pastor Ken DeHart, who read my first manuscript for this book and offered his insight, wisdom, and guidance.

To so many pastors and fellow members of Celebration Church in Georgetown, Texas, for welcoming this prodigal home.

Finally, to my fellow trial lawyers: warriors for justice—I dedicate this work to the struggle that you embrace and suffer with every single day for clients for whom you sacrifice so much, to a public who scorns your very existence.

And to you—yes, you—whom I've not had the privilege, yet, to meet. Thank you for taking the time to read my story. I am truly honored that you spent some of your valuable life reading about my own. Your support means the world to me, and I'd love to invite you to join me on the rest of this journey @**beherostrongnow**! Please invite everyone you know to join the cause of spreading God's hope and light to those who cannot continue to face the weight of their own life's journey alone at **beherostrong.org**. Together, we can lead others to the light that can save them.

To each of you, I ask that you gift yourself the goal of living each day in the fullness of God's love, as best as you can—no matter what pain or hardships may plague your seconds, minutes, hours, or even days. Know that no matter how dark or difficult the challenge—however unlikely or impossible a better tomorrow may seem—that you hold the power to rise above it! By saying no to what hurts us—by calling out to God for help—we are not defeated. Instead, like the mythical, mystical, majestic phoenix, only then are we are able to pull ourselves out of the ashes, transformed—reborn—finally able to fly free in the love of Jesus Christ!

If you or someone you know is ever stuck in the dark or need assistance, please don't hesitate to contact me at **todd@beherostrong.org**.

Before you turn over this page, I ask that you take a quick second to take the pledge to #**BeHeroStrong** today—simply vow to never let whatever weight or failure you carry on your shoulders submerge you into darkness but look to the Father to help you rise above it—do it for yourself, your family, your friends—do it for all of those who choose to leave this Earth before finding their own "phoenix wings" at beherostrong.org/pledge.

Finally, your review of this book at **bit.ly/powerwithinbookrevie w** would be greatly appreciated. Thank you!

#BeHeroStrong

Love,

Todd

The Author

Lawyer by day, author by night, L. Todd Kelly began his practice in the law as a U.S. Marine, achieving the rank of Major. Todd left the Corps to enter private practice in '98, where he represented asbestos exposure victims, birth injury victims, and survivors of nursing home abuse.

In 2006, Todd opened The Kelly Law Firm, in Houston, where he took on the famed Jamie Leigh Jones' sexual assault case against the world's largest private military contractors, Halliburton and Kellogg, Brown & Root. He was featured on 20/20, The Rachel Maddow Show, The New York Times, Wall Street Journal, CNN, NBC, FOX, and was highlighted in the Sundance Film Festival and HBO documentary film, Hot Coffee.

In 2009, Todd appeared in front of committees of the United States Congress and spoke on the Fairness in Arbitration Act in an effort to eliminate mandatory, binding, pre-dispute, secret arbitration provisions that are found in consumer products and other contracts. Todd was consulted by Senator Al Franken, who sponsored an amendment to the Senate Appropriations bill which led to the abolition of forced arbitration for victims of sexual assault by most military contractors.

Since that time, Todd has gone on to be inducted into the Texas Lawyer Hall of Fame following a seventeen-million-dollar verdict and has been interviewed on various legal topics by numerous national and local news programs, including CBS' Insider Edition, receiving the honorary title of "Super Lawyer" and numerous other awards for his legal skills and literary finesse.

Todd is also married to his loving wife, Robbye. Together they have a daughter, Selby Jewel, and they spend time almost weekly with Todd's other children, Joshua, Meghan, and Matthew.

Most importantly in his life, Todd is a child of a loving, forgiving God!

Back at Work: Austin, Texas—2021

About

Crushed by the weight of a major public trial loss, nationally-known and acclaimed trial lawyer, L. Todd Kelly, sits captive in a closet with a gun in his mouth, wondering whether or not his life is even worth living. Deep down, he knows his lust for power, sex, and fame brought him to this day—not to mention the twelve million dollar debt and divorce looming over his head. To escape, he must battle his demons and find the strength to take another breath and choose to live. But will he ever regain his reputation, family's trust, or any ounce of self-respect? *The Power Within* explores one man's journey through sin, marital failure, public loss, and redemption—and will leave you gripped with the inescapable truth about what true power really is.

www.ingramcontent.com/pod-product-compliance
Lightning Source LLC
Chambersburg PA
CBHW070945150426
42812CB00067B/3313/J